# ENDORSEMENTS

"Traveling to Israel with Delores Topliff was my best trip ever! Her experience paved the way to visit unique sites at our own pace and schedule. It was a memorable trip I hope to repeat in the near future."

— PATRICIA BRADLEY, AUTHOR

"Previewing *A Traveling Grandma's Guide to Israel: Adventures, Wit, and Wisdom* before my imminent trip to the Holy Land, came at the perfect time! Delores Topliff's delightful travel book is a treasure for those heading to Israel. This entertaining, informative handbook is essential for exploring such a fascinating country. It let me add unfamiliar things to my list. She is spot on with her advice and information!"

— SALLY SUTTON WILLIARD, WORLD TRAVELER

"Delores Topliff has an organic understanding of Israel that she joyfully shares with fellow travelers. Nothing is overlooked.

Sights, sounds, smells, textures, relationships are all part of the shared experience. Every geographic feature has a name and story that she knows, and every community has a history that shapes the present. Not like a teacher but like a friend, Delores effortlessly transfers her knowledge of and love for Israel to all who want to learn."

— JUDY GLENN, REAL ESTATE BROKER AND WORLD TRAVELER

# A TRAVELING GRANDMA'S GUIDE TO ISRAEL:

## ADVENTURES, WIT, AND WISDOM

By
Delores Topliff

A Traveling Grandma's Guide to Israel: Adventures, Wit, and Wisdom Copyright © 2023 by Delores E. Topliff

Published by TrueNorth Publishing

8985 - 130th Street; Milaca, Minnesota 56353 www.truenorthpublishingdt.com

eBook ISBN: 978-1-7376048-6-0

Paperback ISBN: 978-1-7376048-2-2

ALL RIGHTS RESERVED

No part of this text is allowed to be reproduced or transmitted by any means, whether electronic or mechanical, without the written permission of the author.

Cover Design: Book Marketing Graphics

Interior Design: Cheryl Barr

Map Graphic Contributor: Bardocz Peter / Alamy Stock Vector

*Dedicated to Tina and Moshe, Hava, Jill, Yasmin, Ora, and more. I'm grateful for my many friends in Israel. Your friendships have furnished the experiences and insights told in this book.*

# CONTENTS

| | |
|---|---|
| *Acknowledgments* | ix |
| 1. PACK YOUR BAGS | 1 |
| Why Travel to Israel? How I Got There the First Time | 3 |
| Is it Safe? | 8 |
| First Impressions, Safety Tips, and Travel Tips | 10 |
| Things To Do | 21 |
| Things Not To Do | 22 |
| Dee's Insider Savings Tips | 23 |
| 2. BEFORE YOU GO | 25 |
| Passports, Visas, and Other Travel Documents | 25 |
| Health and Medical Tips | 28 |
| Finances, Transportation, and Accommodations | 32 |
| *Transportation Choices* | 36 |
| Accommodation Options | 47 |
| Volunteer and Educational Opportunities | 56 |
| Main Travel Choices After Landing in Tel Aviv | 63 |
| Israel's National Parks, Historic Sites, and Nature Reserves | 68 |
| Religious Sites | 68 |
| Branches of Judaism, Government, Cultural Explanations | 83 |
| Things to Do | 99 |
| Things Not to Do | 100 |
| Dee's Insider Savings Tips | 102 |
| 3. USEFUL KNOWLEDGE | 105 |
| Israel's People and Primary Religions | 105 |
| Israel's Main Religions–Judaism, Christianity, Islam, Baha'i, and Druze | 107 |
| Government System and Statistics | 112 |
| Things to Do | 114 |
| Things Not to Do | 114 |
| Dee's Insider Savings Tips | 115 |

| | |
|---|---|
| 4. THINGS TO SEE AND DO | 117 |
| Israel's Geography and Major Destinations | 117 |
| Once You're in the Land and on Your Way | 121 |
| Prolonged Stays and Living Abroad | 122 |
| Major Destinations Alphabetically | 134 |
| Things to Do | 145 |
| Things Not To Do | 146 |
| 5. DON'T MISS OUT | 147 |
| Major Religious Events | 147 |
| Religious Events | 153 |
| Things to Do | 156 |
| Things Not To Do | 156 |
| 6. OFF THE BEATEN PATH | 157 |
| *Hidden Gems and Recommended Tours and Organizations* | |
| Recommended Tours, Organizations, YouTube Features | 159 |
| Things to Do | 159 |
| Things Not to Do | 160 |
| 7. HEADING HOME | 161 |
| Special Keepsakes | 161 |
| Departing Flights | 162 |
| Things To Do | 162 |
| Things Not To Do | 163 |
| 8. KEEPING ISRAEL ALIVE WITH YOU | 165 |
| 9. ISRAEL'S WONDERFUL BEST-LOVED FOODS AND RECIPES | 167 |
| Rich cultural experience is gained through enjoying local and national foods | 168 |
| Things To Do | 190 |
| Things Not To Do | 190 |
| *Addendum* | 191 |
| *More of Delores Topliff's books* | 197 |
| *From the Author* | 203 |

# ACKNOWLEDGMENTS

I'm thankful most of all to the Lord who opened unexpected doors to let me visit Israel the first time and has kept me returning ever since.

Warm thanks to Julie Gwinn, Vice President and Agent with The Seymour Agency—for great encouragement.

Also to Elisa Houot, agent with The Seymour Agency—for perfect questions and enthusiasm.

I'm rich in friendships and PR expertise with Liana George and Danielle Hoover, brilliant cornerstones of The Author's Write Hand team.

I'm thankful for those who've traveled in Israel with me and for the amazing people we've met there who've become friends over the last thirty-nine years. It's an incredibly rich journey that isn't ending.

I appreciate expert formatter and wearer of many hats, Cheryl Barr, who has worked long and patiently on this project and all the others with me.

Thanks to my KCW mentoring friends who've read parts of this book in many stages, and to highly valued author friends who encourage daily.

Thanks to Jenny Myers of Jenny's Audio, former college student and current esteemed professional. It's a joy to see all stages of your journey.

Special thanks to proofreaders extraordinaire Nancy Williams and Mike Topliff, PhD. You make my work shine.

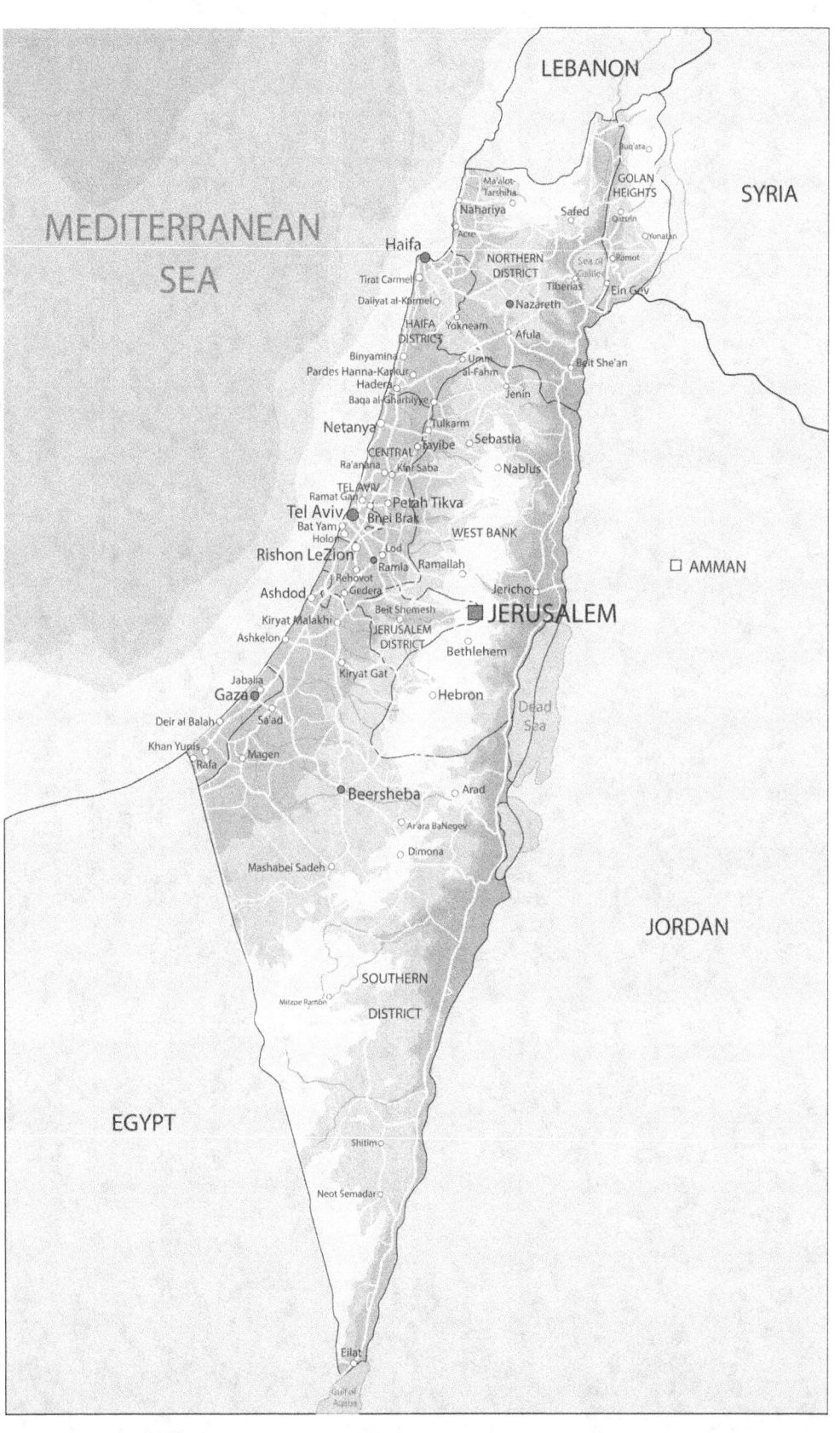

# 1

## PACK YOUR BAGS

During his lifetime, humorist Mark Twain was best known as a travel writer. His 1869 top seller, *Innocents Abroad,* described his jaunts around Europe and the Mediterranean, including Israel, where he, "adventured like Huckleberry Finn." Later he wrote, "Travel is fatal to prejudice, bigotry, and narrow-mindedness, and many of our people need it sorelyBroad, wholesome, charitable views of men and things cannot be acquired by vegetating in one little corner of the earth all one's lifetime."

These days, travel isn't only for young, fit, poor backpackers. People don't have to be rich or in perfect health to enjoy foreign trips. Travel benefits everyone—even grandmas on retirement incomes with stiff knees. It expands our horizons and makes us better citizens in our world. This book shares proven tips on how to be safe, economize, and enjoy wonderful, memorable trips to Israel.

When trips are not possible, like during global pandemics, readers of all ages can enjoy the vivid and interesting travel stories included here and feel like they have taken actual journeys, too! May this book encourage many readers to start planning their own trips.

I love learning and have university degrees, but travel is my favorite form of education. After enjoying one hundred and thirty-five days in Israel during nine lengthy trips over thirty-nine years, I consider Israel the most unique, fascinating nation I've visited on four continents. There, ancient history intersects with modern-day accomplishments and fills in blanks on many other categories in between. On each of my visits, I've found new things to delight in. An added bonus is that most people in the nation speak and understand English.

Israel is so much more than the familiar best-known sites, those seen in classic postcard photos and on glossy calendars. I encourage travelers to read this book and plan and then visit and discover Israel for yourselves.

Young people, Baby Boomers, and/or seniors—we're all exactly the right age to travel in today's world with confidence! Expense should not keep us home. The financial tips I share make trips affordable. Travel costs for friends accompanying me these days usually run around $120 U.S. per day after airfare or less. That includes housing, car rental, gasoline, most site admissions, and breakfasts. It does not include other meals, souvenirs, or shopping splurges. With actual costs managed well, the remaining questions are, where to travel? When? And with whom?

For me, the answer to where to travel is Israel. When? Any time you can. With whom? Those who love this informative, economical trip style.

To plan my first journey, I read piles of books, wrote letters, and collected facts but found little on how to cut costs or simplify travel. On each of my nine trips so far, I've gained much additional information, and my tips work.

Whether readers visit Israel on organized tours, or research and plan trips alone or with friends, the information presented in *A Traveling Grandma's Guide to Israel: Adventures, Wit, and Wisdom* equips them to transform their travel dreams into affordable realities. Our curiosity and genuine interest in the land endears us to its residents. Almost all people you encounter in Israel wish to help and answer questions. They easily become friends.

If preferred, it's possible to hire a personal guide for a few hours or days at any specific destination. To do so, contact the registry of government-licensed Israeli tour guides or any listed at these online sites: Israel Ministry of Tourism; touristisrael.com; tripadvisor.com, etc.

**Why Travel to Israel? How I Got There the First Time**

To date, I have visited thirty-six nations throughout North and South America, Europe, and Asia but find Israel the most unique and fascinating destination of all. *Synergy* is the word to describe the results when the sum of individual parts added together is greater than the total of them separately. To me, that describes Israel as visitors encounter the unforgettable scenes and experiences that combine to create the rich takeaways of any trip.

It's not necessary to travel through Israel on highly organized, tightly scheduled expensive tours. While those typically provide comfortable door-to-door service to the best-known sites, most cannot include everything and leave little time for meaningful interactions with the nation and its people.

The beauty of Israel goes far beyond the standard inspiring sacred and/or tourist stops. I enjoy its vast and varied panorama and sweeping landscapes. My nine lengthy trips so far mean I have now driven from border towns in the far north to the southern tip joining Egypt and the Red Sea as well as to most points in between. On my eighth trip, I drove over 650 miles crisscrossing the nation and taking time to search out lesser-known destinations. In many ways, that was my best trip yet. Schedule enough time to broaden your focus and add extras. You'll be glad you did.

The human connections matter. I love spending quality time in each location. Since planning my first open-ended journey to Israel in 1984, during a summer break from college teaching, I have carefully planned each of my own trips. Now friends and even strangers ask me to help them plan theirs. They love the results.

Many people I met during that first thirty-six-day trip to Israel have remained friends. We stay in touch, and I love seeing them each time I return. During periods when I can't be there, we connect on WhatsApp or in Zoom meetings. The places seen and experiences gained are like high interest-bearing deposits in my personal bank account of rich travel memories.

Don't let anyone tell you that planning personal travel can't be done or that it is hard to do. It's not. It's even fun, and you'll love the results. Imagine selecting and poring over maps, checking your budget, and then using your calendar to schedule a route with destinations unique to you and possibly your friends' interests. Before departing, because of your hard work, you'll know what to expect when you get there to maximize your top-quality experience in each location.

This is how the professional travelers do it. But, be forewarned. After you enjoy even one truly excellent travel experience, you'll find it addictive. You'll save money and make plans to come again to learn and enjoy even more about Israel or any country. It may be time to begin planning your trip now.

Here's one experience that deepened my love for Israel. Years ago, my husband and I moved from the West Coast to Toronto, Canada where he pursued a Master's degree and I finished my undergraduate work. I didn't know that University College which I enrolled in inside the University of Toronto had around a ninety percent Jewish enrollment. As an English and History major, I took a required course on John Milton's *Paradise Lost* and *Paradise Regained*.

Familiar with both epic poems, I easily answered questions, but eight female Jewish students, used to earning A's, were floundering. After class one day, all eight met me in the hall and asked if I would teach them the foundations of Christianity so they could understand Milton and do better in class. I agreed.

We began eating lunch together and formed lasting friendships. Some of us have stayed in touch all through the years. Even after my family moved to the U.S., we visited Toronto again at times, and two of those students have visited us. One of them, Florence Goldstein Rubin Barik, consistently stayed in touch. Our children also enjoyed occasional visits. After many years passed, Florence was widowed and moved to Israel. We had a great reunion in October 2014, when I had led five other travelers throughout Israel for two weeks. Imagine my joy when Florence was free to meet me at a stone bench just outside Jaffa Gate. It had been ages since we'd seen each other. I walked to the Old City fast that morning and was welcomed by a smiling lady wearing blue standing and calling my name.

"Delores?"

"Yes!"

After many years, daughters of two faiths hugged each other and enjoyed a day together again. Part of my love for Israel grew from our early university days, and Florence says our friendship has deepened her faith. She has now returned to her family in Canada but still visits Israel occasionally. Every time I pass Jaffa Gate, I think of meeting Florence there and always hope to find her there again.

Here are my top reasons for visiting Israel (in no special order):

- Israel is rich in ancient history and earns international acclaim for its medical, scientific, and technical contributions to today's world. Many say today Israel is stepping into its destiny.
- Israel has vital spiritual importance as the hub of three major world religions and is the birthplace of Judaism and Christianity.
- Israel's population blends fascinating people from many cultural backgrounds and languages. Most speak and understand English.
- Israel offers world-class art and culture in a great variety of venues, genres, and expressions.

- Israel's geography provides breathtaking calendar-worthy natural beauty. Definitely bring whichever technology best permits you to capture treasured recordings, videos, and pictures.
- Israel contains seven of the world's thirteen climate zones which allows visitors to enjoy their preferred temperatures year-round. (Who doesn't love finding carpets of wild daffodils, narcissi, and cyclamen blooming across northern Israel in shades of yellows, white, and pink—even in January?) One person didn't accompany our January 2023 trip because she read online that January in Israel can be cold and rainy. We went anyway and enjoyed lots of sunshine and got suntans. Our daily temperatures from January 7th to 21st, 2023, often reached 65-67 F. The predicted rains were occasional light mists except for one 20-30 minute period when it actually rained at the archaeology site we were visiting in the Negev Desert where all local literature said it never rains. We enjoyed the experience.
- Israel leads the world in military and security preparedness. Their outstanding emergency responders are counted among the world's best. They frequently assist other nations facing national disasters like earthquakes, raging fires, and major health crises including disease outbreaks.
- El Al planes possess missile defense systems. That airline is considered one of the world's safest for its outstanding security procedures on the ground and in the air.
- Israel welcomes visitors from around the world and appreciates North American travelers because of our recognition of and support for their existence as a nation.
- U.S. and Canadian currencies and credit cards are welcomed and easily used.
- Most world nations maintain embassies in Israel. The country also hosts a NATO and UN Security base for

added security. So far, I have not registered with the U.S. Consulate or other foreign countries when visiting Israel, but some say it is wise to do so and easily done.

A 2020 editorial in the *Daily Health Post* states, "Scientists Say That Traveling Makes Us Much Happier Than Any Material Wealth." Many people shop the moment they have money in their pocket, but those purchases only bring temporary happiness that "begins to fade" immediately. "Lasting happiness only comes from meaningful connections. Traveling links us to (enriching) cultures and places.... Our brain and body become keen to absorb new information."

I fully agree. Travel benefits us all in countless ways.

Every journey has a starting point. Most first-born children in families face challenges but also enjoy added opportunities. We grow up fast. After learning to help with household chores, I spent hours in the public library across the street from our house always reading at least one book daily—but often more. In grade school, I devoured *National Geographic* and *Holiday* Magazines and mailed off the reply cards inside to embassies and travel agencies offering free booklets and brochures. I loved receiving mail from distant places. Plus, the materials received raised my school grades.

In fact, World Geography is still a university class I teach, and my love for travel continues and grows. I also teach History of Ancient Israel which adds to my further enjoyment of that land. Otherwise, no one in our family had traveled much except for my father who served in the U.S. Navy overseas and introduced me to books written by explorers to equatorial Africa.

It is generally considered safer and more fun to travel with companions than alone. However, I comfortably go on my own when necessary and enjoy meeting fellow travelers. To date, flying alone to Singapore and on to Indonesia was my greatest and longest solo journey. Other than one major glitch that caused an international airline to gift me many air miles and buy my replacement dress for a very formal Indonesian wedding attended by six thousand guests because my luggage was delayed for five days, that trip ended well.

More than 23,000 readers of my Trip Advisor posts have found my tips helpful. Delighted in 2019 to visit my favorite Tel Aviv-Jaffa restaurant with friends, I told our server how happy I was to enjoy their beautiful location and atmosphere again. I gushed that I had awarded them high praise on Trip Advisor but expected nothing in return. Moments later our hostess reappeared carrying a silver tray holding pink bubbly drinks in crystal glasses.

"These are for you on the house with our thanks," she said. "This is passion fruit, guava, pomegranate, and a splash of something more."

We enjoyed the refreshment, and I later wrote another positive review on Trip Advisor. Most businesses and travel destinations wish to please the public and earn top ratings.

This book's travel tips contain lessons gleaned during my nine trips to Israel over nearly forty years. I had scheduled a trip in 2020 until Covid and variant pandemic restrictions made that impossible. I was happy to complete another 15-day trip in January 2023. The compiled information offered here helps readers plan and enjoy their own usually trouble-free experiences. No matter your age, travel is possible and fun. I keep my passport up to date and urge my friends to do the same. You never know when the next trip opportunity may arise. Be ready!

**Is it Safe?**

People say, "We hear of conflicts, tear gas, and bombings. Is it safe to travel in Israel?" Based on my 135 days there during nine trips in over thirty-nine years, my traveling friends and I say a resounding "Yes!"

In 2017, the *New York Times* published an article titled, "Why Israel has the most technologically advanced military on Earth." It said, "Israel is one of the world's top weapons exporters with $6.5

billion in annual arms sales. Since 1985, they are also the world's largest exporter of drones."

The Israeli Defense Forces (IDF) is presently considered the world's leader in security. We see male and female soldiers carrying Uzis everywhere to keep things safe. That reassures us, and they make it look easy. I've been in Israel twice when bombs have fallen in the country but IDF jets flying overhead made us feel protected—not endangered.

Touristisrael.com says, "Despite what you see in the news, Israel is actually a very secure country. The main tourist areas, Tel Aviv, Jerusalem, Haifa, the Negev, the Dead Sea, and the Galilee, remain as safe as always."

On my 2019 trip, as friends and I neared the end of the Via Dolorosa in Jerusalem's Old City, three armed IDF soldiers in combat gear dashed past us over cobblestones toward the Lions' Gate which opens directly into the Muslim Quarter just beyond. We heard no follow-up shouts or shots, but those soldiers meant business and moved so fast they were a thundering blur. Israel's military and police professionals do their best to maintain order and keep vigilance, so tensions do not escalate.

Israeli law now requires that all new buildings include reinforced security "safe rooms" in their structure. This is because some years have seen rockets fired into Israel from Gaza, Syria or Lebanon, but seldom with damaging hits or casualties. Safe rooms are comfortable for short-term stays in the event a rocket is launched without adequate warning for people to reach a public bomb shelter. I know few people who have personally had to use them. I definitely don't know anyone injured in such an attack. Their use may be like the adage, "If you carry an umbrella, it won't rain."

In the unlikely event that on a trip to Israel anyone on your trip is hurt or needs assistance of any kind, almost any stranger would assist or direct you to the help needed. Most Israeli residents are welcoming, helpful, and appreciative of visitors. At the same time, do pay attention to your inner sensitivity. Occasional problems can arise anywhere.

Not only in Israel, but across North America and in all nations today, safety-consciousness matters. Signs like these remind us of common-sense guidelines:

- Stay alert and aware of surroundings.
- Report suspicious persons or activities.
- Report unattended packages.

**First Impressions, Safety Tips, and Travel Tips**

During the last minutes of my first-ever flight from London's Heathrow Airport to Israel in June 1984, I peered through my plane's window into pre-dawn darkness until my eyes ached. For years, I'd looked forward to this moment. Finally, I could distinguish the Mediterranean's long dark coastline from lighter white-capped waves pounding the shore.

The land of the Bible remained dark until sparkles began to outline Tel Aviv. A single knife blade of silver light slashed the horizon, dividing the black sky above from the swirling water beneath as Israel's orange sun rose to unveil the coast. Breakers rushing to shore fell back in white foam. Finally, Tel Aviv's landscape emerged, bordered by corridors of graceful palm trees. At last, our plane touched down, and I soon discovered why visitors feel strangely at home.

All of my advance planning paid off because the couple we would stay with for our days in Jerusalem had told us what transportation to use, how to locate it, and how to reach their home where the husband would pay the driver the right amount in the correct currency. We were well-connected and off to a great start, but more about that later.

∼

*A Traveling Grandma's Guide to Israel*

## How My First Trip to Israel Developed

I was born in Washington State but married a Canadian, which made me a citizen of two countries. I liked having international flavor in my life. Education has also always mattered to me. After our family moved to northern British Columbia, Canada, I joined others in developing a good small college that met provincial guidelines. We offered basic classes and then developed a fuller course catalog. Someone suggested we teach Bible Archaeology. I love learning, so I volunteered for that assignment. As I began preparation, the only materials I had were the archaeology section at the back of a Thompson Chain Bible and a paperback on sale on the subject from Religious Book Discount House.

A month later, a retired Biblical Archaeologist accompanied the sister of our college director on a visit. In 1964, Robert (Bob) Allen had begun a ten-year journey through thirty-nine European nations and the Middle East. He spent seven years in Israel without returning to the U.S. During that time, he collected artifacts to establish the ten-room Prewitt-Allen Archaeological Museum in Corban (Baptist) College in Salem, Oregon.

Our college director suggested I tell Bob I would be teaching the class.

"Don't you dare," I said, embarrassed to have so little material to work with. Of course, she did tell him. Bob asked to see what I had. Instead of laughing, he asked if I would let him send us books, color slides, replica artifacts, and even a few genuine originals. I assured him we would be very grateful.

The day came when his large insured box arrived by mail. His letter in advance had explained what would be inside. At mid-morning school break, I gathered our elementary, junior high, high school, and college students together. They crowded around as I knelt and undid the wrappings to lift out the treasures inside. Our favorites were the two-thousand-year-old earthenware oil lamps small enough to hold in a hand, like those described in the Matthew 25 Parable of the Ten Virgins.

As I removed bubble wrap and exposed the clay items to air, we inhaled the good earthy smell of ancient Israel. The children were ecstatic. Their eyes shone. Soot lines marked where the lamps had last been filled and burned. Bob had told me to buy cotton wicks and olive oil to light them. No one breathed as I struck a match and the flame caught, its golden light bringing Bible scenes to life once again.

Bob also included a genuine earthenware water flask to be worn at the waist hung by a woven grass cord from the time of the prophet Samuel plus a larger earthenware juglet from the days of King Saul.

With these wonderful materials and more on hand, I taught a series of evening Archaeology classes that nearby communities attended. Bob flew north to be present but refused my suggestion that he teach instead. He wanted my skills developed to extend his knowledge to others. Next, he donated $3,000 to our college if I would travel to Rome, Athens, and Israel to explore ancient sites, collect more artifacts, and return home better prepared to teach archaeology. I had a year to plan that trip. Planning and research increases the joy of the trip itself!

Friends thought I shouldn't take that first lengthy trip alone. Mutual friends introduced me to Cindy, a young bookkeeper in town, who had just broken off an ill-suited engagement. She had savings and needed something new in her life. The timing was perfect. We got acquainted and she bought a ticket. We had a great trip and have stayed friends ever since.

### Safety Tips—Travel Smart and Fit in Like a Local

My earlier international trip had involved staying three-and-a-half months in Colombia, South America helping a network of jungle mission schools and teachers. Based near Colombia's borders with Peru and Ecuador, I also reached schools along the Caquetá River, a tributary of the Amazon, by dugout canoe. In beautiful primitive settings, I wrote curriculum, presented teacher training, and administered student achievement tests. We caught and ate piranhas instead of the piranhas eating us.

My younger son, Aaron, then age fourteen, came with me. My sixteen-year-old son, Andrew, didn't feel designed for jungle heat. We kept in touch with him by ham radio where and when we could. Friends suggested that in Florencia, the last large town before leaving civilization, Aaron and I meet ninety-year-old Don Pedro Arisa. That lively gentleman had spent ten years working in New York City earning money to purchase and bring back the only soft-ice-cream machine in his region. He welcomed us warmly and shared travel survival tips that work anywhere.

"People will try to rob you," he warned. "Whether you ride a jeep or bus, whenever it stops, get off and make sure your luggage isn't intentionally given to someone else." He reached into his pocket, pulling out something shiny.

"The best protection against theft is a pair of scissors. When someone tries to rob you, stab their hand with the pointed ends, like this."

He jabbed, and we jumped. "It works everywhere, even in New York City." He smiled broadly.

He liked the two-quart stainless steel thermos I brought for our safe water supply.

"You're smart to carry that. It's another good weapon," he said. "My thermos has many dents with a story behind each one." Don Pedro's survival tips work well.

In Israel, five years later, Dutchwoman, Tina Goldenberg, was equally savvy in making us wise travelers. As a child, she attended Corrie ten Boom's girls' Bible class. After serving as a missionary nurse in Brazil for six years, Tina returned to The Netherlands and from there made thirty successful Bible smuggling trips for Open Doors, Brother Andrew's organization. Andrew's full name is Andrew van der Bijl. For those who don't know his remarkable story and ministry, his biography, *God's Smuggler,* is also a great movie. He passed away in September 2022, leaving an astounding legacy. Learn more at https://www.opendoorsusa.org/

During her daring Bible smuggling trips into Eastern European nations where distributing Bibles was forbidden, Tina developed outstanding safety guidelines which she shared with us—the best I've heard. For example, she taught us to remove the collar from a dress, blouse, or shirt and stitch three sides closed leaving one narrow edge open to stuff currency or vital papers in. (For those unwilling to sacrifice a garment collar, buy something inexpensive at a thrift store.) Slide currency, maps, or paperwork into the long narrow space. Females can pin the collar to the bottom front of their bras for quick access when needed. Males can pin or snap theirs to the bottom of shirts or inside the waistband of shorts or slacks. We also sewed small lightweight cloth bags to carry passports and tickets in and hung those from a shoelace or cord around our necks.

Former mystery writer, John D. MacDonald, gave this added tip to people needing to carry cash or identity papers. "Buy long Ace bandages for trick knees. Divide the cash or papers in half. Wrap each pile in clear plastic. Slip items under the bandage above the knee in front and above the knee in back. If necessary, buy two bandages for both knees. This is comfortable with no risk of losing."

It only takes moments to find a private spot to access needed items. However, when in England touring the Tower of London, I stepped into what I believed was a private alcove behind a wrought iron spiral staircase. While retrieving my cash, I spotted a well-hidden video camera scanning the area. After unintentionally entertaining a surprised video security officer, I blushed and beat a hasty retreat.

Helping us navigate Israel like the locals, Tina taught us to dress inconspicuously and follow more tips: Carry a nondescript shopping bag on our shoulders to look like local housewives buying groceries instead of vulnerable gawking tourists. Stash phones, tape recorders, cameras, and/or billfolds inside such bags. Tucked in but not visible in my shoulder bag, I kept my tape recorder turned on to capture joyful bells ringing from ancient churches or Muslim muezzins calling the faithful to prayer from the minarets of mosques. It's wise to keep purses or bags with straps over one's head and shoulder instead of just over one's shoulder where it can be pulled off. When sitting in restaurants or anywhere, place purses or bags between your feet for maximum safety control.

Tina led us into the back rooms of jewelry stores where favorable currency rates were given. She taught us that vendors like buyers to haggle or counteroffer. "It's less fun for them if we simply pay full price," she said. Every day, we learned more.

Here, I'll share a scary experience while giving thanks that so far my life mishaps have ended well. One thing archaeologist Bob Allen asked me to buy with the trip funds he provided was a Pontius Pilate coin for our college studies. That low denomination bronze *prutah* issued by Pilate between 26 and 36 AD/CE holds interest for Christians and Jews.

There are wide-ranging views regarding Pilate as Procurator—some consider him outstanding, a man who became a Christian and started a church on his Italian country estate once he retired. Others including the Roman historian Philo accuse him of being "inflexible, merciless and obstinate" to the Jewish people. The truth may lie in between, but in issuing coins, Pilate avoided offending the Jews by stamping barley ears or a shepherd's crook on one side of coins and the umbrella-like canopy of rule on the other instead of portraying the emperor's head.

At any rate, Bob asked me to find and buy one—easily done online today—but not in 1984 on that first trip. Much of Israel is an active archaeological site. Proposed road and construction projects must be inspected and approved by the Israel Antiquities Authority (IAA) before going forward. The IAA legally owns all artifacts found anywhere in Israel including underwater sites. The Antiquities Law passed in 1978 forbids the sale of any items man-made before 1700 AD/CE. The only exception is items already in authorized antiquities shops' inventory" before the 1978 law. Legal sales come with certificates of authenticity usually displayed in the windows of reliable antiquities shops.

I didn't know all that then. The process is more regulated now. Cindy and I visited several Old City shops. They offered plentiful handblown Roman glass two thousand years old with its shimmering patina (which I love), ancient pottery pieces and shards that it's possible to approximately date by material and design, and Roman, Maccabean, and Hasmonean period coins—but no Pontius Pilate *prutah*.

Without distinguishing whether we were in Jewish or Arab-run shops, we met a proprietor who quoted a fair price and said, "I have a beautiful specimen at my home. Come." He headed for the back door and waved for us to follow.

Looking back, a wiser option might have been to request that he bring the coin to his shop the next day. I imagine that during the Intifada with poor sales, he wanted to be sure of a sale in preferred U.S. currency. He opened the shop's back door and ushered us into the back seat of a large black car. As I began realizing this might not be a great idea, he drove out of the Old City into the largely Arab neighborhood of Silwan (Siloam in the Bible) nearby or perhaps closer to the sometimes agitated mixed Jewish-Arab Abu Tor area to its south. I did my best to keep track of turns and street signs (in Hebrew) in case we had to find our way back. We didn't have cell phones. Within minutes, we entered the underground garage of his multi-story cement block home and climbed stairs to a nicely furnished living area.

At first the shopkeeper was all business, showing us a good bona fide Pontius Pilate coin plus other genuine artifacts, but I only had funds for the *prutah*. He soon realized we were not rich Americans. (I am American by birth but also Canadian by marriage. I love the U.S. but it's sometimes beneficial to travel as a Canadian, as they are often viewed as less wealthy and less confrontational.)

As soon as the man received my payment, he called to his wife, "Fatima, bring refreshments."

She instantly appeared. Fairly young, gracious, dressed beautifully in an attractive flowing garment, she served hot sweet, spiced tea and the most delectable date-filled cookies I had ever tasted.

She and Cindy and I chatted briefly. I was reassured, having heard that although animosity can exist between Arabs and North Americans, if we are in their homes as guests, our safety is assured. I told the shopkeeper we had an appointment soon to meet a friend at Jaffa Gate and asked him to take us there.

"Not there," he said, "but I will take you to Lions' Gate." That is near the Dome of the Rock and connects the Muslim

Quarter to the Old City, which left us some distance to walk but was a decent compromise. True to his word, he deposited us safely. I'm thankful this experience ended well, but realize it was risky and unwise. I have never repeated that particular type of adventure again.

**Fond Remembrances of Israel Keep Me Returning**

Regarding travel, Buddhism's Dalai Lama advises, "Once a year, go someplace you've never been before." That's sound advice. But the amazing thing is, even though I have visited Israel multiple times, returning there is always like going somewhere new. Along with the key sites I'm eager to revisit and show others, I add a few fresh locations to each trip plus leave time for unexpected opportunities to make new travel experience memories.

When Cindy and I made our first trip to Israel, we sometimes had unusual and unexplained help finding our way. Some who came to our aid seemed to be such divine encounters, we wondered if our helpers were more than human. We felt that angels had helped us find our way. In Eilat, as we got off the bus and began walking with our suitcases, a nicely dressed young man approached us and said, "You're going to The Shelter; follow me." We were and we did.

Weeks later as we rode a city bus in Jaffa (Joppa, Yafo), a smiling middle-aged blonde woman, dressed in blue and white clothing who looked like she might be Dutch, walked up to us and said, "This is your stop for Beit Immanuel. You need to get off here and follow me." Again, we did, and she led us exactly to where we were going.

It was wonderful to experience such care on that first trip. I have come to rely on and expect such divine intervention each time we've needed it. Of course, the Lord also reminds us to use good sense.

On our November 2019 trip, when a friend bravely using a crutch and brace had difficulty walking, I made sure we did more driving than walking to explore. That meant seeing Safed in Northern Galilee for the first time as well as lovely new-to-us places throughout the Judean hill country. Now that I've discovered additional sites, plus a small town with a fabulous Arab restaurant, we'll go again and explore further. We meet delightful helpful people everywhere along the way. Little did we know that a week after we completed our trip, Covid would close Israel and many countries to international travel.

To get maximum benefit from trips, research and plan well in advance of departure dates. Wise planning adds anticipation and helps ensure that nothing crucial is overlooked.

While traveling, take lots of photos. For the wisdom of not letting the public know when travelers are away, some prefer to wait until they return home to post them but should write or dictate detailed notes and label photographs with accurate information to add to trip reports later. Record-keeping activities are one of the last steps in completing wonderful travel adventures and preserving memories.

In fact, you may be asked to share proven travel tips with friends and acquaintances, as I now often am, to help others plan their adventures as well. Some who've gone with me have voluntarily written endorsements saying it was their best travel experience ever. That's how this book came about. I find all aspects of travel from initial planning to trip completion are fun and memorable parts of the travel process.

While I cannot guarantee this result, one widowed grandmother who visited Israel for the first time with my 2019 trip posted happy travel photos on Facebook. For years, Teresa and her husband had socialized with another couple until that man's wife passed away. The remaining three people drifted apart, and then Teresa's husband died. Years passed until the widower noticed Teresa's happy Israel travel posts on Facebook and friended her. Once she returned home, they ran into each other twice in the same day in a building supply store and again in Walmart. They began spending time together and renewed warm friendship. That Valentine's Day, he proposed. I was delighted to attend their lovely wedding.

All the walking we do sightseeing plus eating healthy fresh Israeli food means that those traveling with me usually lose weight. Two trips ago we averaged walking four to seven miles a day. Two of our eight travelers lost ten pounds each in two weeks. All of us came home lighter and more fit. I tease that I should advertise a weight loss component for future trips and charge extra. That benefit is not experienced by those taking highly organized and much more expensive door-to-door tours. My team members return feeling better than when we left and bring back home Israeli recipes they enjoy preparing at home. I offer some near the end of this printed and Kindle book (but not in the Audio version).

My first trip to Israel was so incredible, I determined to find a way to come again. The land's songs and scenes fill my heart and keep me returning. How can we not love a nation whose capital is known as "Jerusalem of Gold" for how sunset transforms the gorgeous white limestone blocks that build so much of the city into shining gold? A land whose national anthem is "Hatikvah" *the Hope* with a melody based on Smetana's "Moldau." Its translation into English says,

> *As long as within our hearts the Jewish soul sings,*
> *As long as forward to the East to Zion, looks the eye – Our hope is not yet lost, it is two thousand years old,*
> *To be a free people in our land, the land of Zion and Jerusalem.*
> *Israel's unofficial anthem, "Jerusalem of Gold", describes the people's religious devotion and ancient longing to return to their homeland.*
> *As clear as wine, the wind is flying. Among the dreamy pines.*
> *As evening light is slowly dying. And a lonely bell still chimes*
> *So many songs, so many stories . . . And here is the chorus:*
> *But as I sing to you, my city, and you with crowns adorn,*
> *I am the least of all your children, of all the poets born.*
> *Your name will scorch my lips forever, like a seraph's kiss, I'm told,*

> *That song also reminds me of the poignant words in Psalm 137 as If I forget thee, golden city, Jerusalem of gold.*

Israel's people in captivity recall and long for their home. 5 "If I forget thee, O Jerusalem, let my right hand forget her cunning. 6 If I do not remember thee, let my tongue cleave to the roof of my mouth; if I prefer not Jerusalem above my chief joy."

Perhaps because of the horrors of the Holocaust, the Jewish people value family life extremely highly, and tend to pamper their children. Fathers proudly push baby buggies and carry infants in slings across their chests. At age eighteen, Israel's sons and daughters are drafted into the IDF to safeguard the nation and suppress terrorism. Most families know someone who has died in military service.

I remember my first time walking along the Mediterranean shore at dusk near Tel Aviv watching fishermen cast out lines and haul in fish until it was almost too dark to see. Near the spot where Jonah departed on his voyage that ended differently than he planned, fading light revealed concentration camp numbers tattooed in purple on the forearm of an older man. That sight stopped me cold. I understood immediately where and how he got that tattoo.

In growing dusk on that balmy evening, the Holocaust survivor calmly continued casting out his line and reeling in his catch, a man who had survived a greater threat and escape than Jonah. I didn't speak. We never met, but my heart saluted him, thrilled for his freedom and ability to experience life's pleasures now far beyond whether he hooked a fish on his line on that particular evening —or not.

*Shabbat* is Judaism's seventh day of the week for rest and prayer. It begins each Friday evening at sundown and lasts until sundown the next day. As Shabbats (Sabbaths) begin, fathers bring home flowers to enhance the family's dinner table. Following the meal, the fathers and sons go to synagogue to thank God. On returning home, as families reunite, they greet each other and sing Shalom Aleichem, "Peace be upon you," the traditional song sung by Jews everywhere on Friday nights to signal Shabbat's arrival and to welcome the angels accompanying each person home. The peace and rest of Sabbath continues until the stars come out the next day when the next sunset marks the official end of Shabbat.

Whether Israel's citizens are observant Jews or not, the entire nation stills to a pin-drop hush from sundown Friday until sunset Saturday to honor God, family, and the values that matter most. There are almost no sounds of traffic until business resumes on Sunday mornings. During the Sunday through Thursday work week, Israel is noisy and vibrantly alive until its pulse slows again for the shabbat and weekend. After my first visit to Israel years ago, the land's sights, sounds, tastes, fragrances, and touch have remained with me.

Israel is a nation where returning Jews from around the world are welcomed home as residents. The process is called Aliyah, the Law of Return. Irrespective of social or economic status, new arrivals from all nations are received and provided for. I am unaware of any nation offering a better immigration policy process.

**Things To Do**

- Do learn from people you know, books you read, or sites you follow and choose which travel pattern best suits you. Plan your travels accordingly.
- Do plan well to avoid schedule gaps or surprises during your trip.
- Do bring all important papers and ID, including details of medical insurance, etc.

- Do leave things in good order at home and/or leave matters in the hands of trusted family and friends while away so you can minimize concerns and distractions to fully enjoy your trip.
- Do be aware at home or abroad of the best entry and exit points of any location should an emergency arise. Covering contingencies well means trouble-free travel. I have never required medical help in a foreign country, but I know the process to follow if that became necessary.
- In the unlikely event that you're in Israel when military alerts happen, check with locals for protocols to follow. You would hear plenty of advance warning from public media sources and the general public. Friends and I reached Israel on one trip to learn the second Gaza War had just broken out. We stayed informed and knew precautions needed if necessary, but none were. Israel is excellent at informing and protecting their population.

One afternoon years ago when my then young teenage sons and I walked through a deserted part of Vancouver B.C., Canada's waterfront, a man down on his luck eyed my purse and began following us. Without saying a word, my then thirteen and fifteen-year-old sons flanked me on both sides as we doubled our walking speed and left the man behind. As Ian Fleming wrote in James Bond books, "Sometimes during travel, we may notice the same faces, clothing, or vehicles more than once. If that happens twice, it may be coincidence—more than twice? You may have a problem and need to plan and execute an exit strategy."

**Things Not To Do**

- Do not delay planning details to the last minute as a free-spirited traveler assuming everything will work out once you arrive.

- Do not panic if you're ever in any nation when an emergency arises, whether it's a natural disaster, military action, pandemic, etc. Stay calm, get informed, and follow guidelines. Besides keeping yourself and your team safe, you may be able to assist others.
- Do not be *a victim* anywhere. Have a mental plan if any situation seems dangerous. There's nothing wrong with asking strangers for help or screaming if necessary. However, in my many years of travel, I have never witnessed anyone having to do so.

**Dee's Insider Savings Tips**

- Read and research widely before you go to decide which destinations and plans suit you best.
- Secure maps and mark them with the notes of where you want to go and what you want to see at destinations so you arrive safely without incident.
- Travel and accommodation rates are much lower in the off-seasons when smaller crowds give you more of the authentic feel of Israel. If desired, alter your travel dates to experience significant savings.
- Choose your preferred means of transportation and make reservations far enough in advance to receive maximum discounts.
- Know exactly where you want to go and when to be your own tour guide. If desired, consider joining a tour or hiring a recommended guide for only those places and short lengths of time where it may be wise for security reasons or for in-depth insight into special sites. On rare occasions, I have paid for excellent two-hour or half-day tours, but otherwise have enjoyed researching and arranging my own.

- Establish communication with someone in the country, whether it's your accommodation managers, sales staff in local stores, etc., to get the inside track on the best area sites to see as well as to stay informed on any national events that might affect your trip. A grocery clerk in Big Island, Hawaii, once told us about majestic unadvertised sea cliffs at the end of a narrow road that had wonderful views and memories of that island. No road sign pointed to that destination.

## 2

# BEFORE YOU GO

**Passports, Visas, and Other Travel Documents**

For peace of mind, apply for or renew passports far in advance of departure dates. U.S. and Canadian passports typically require six weeks of processing time for issue or renewal. They may be received sooner if applicants pay extra for rushed service but that can be avoided by planning ahead.

Passports are now required for all international travel outside of North America. Less expensive Passport Cards serve as limited travel documents for travel between the U.S. and Canada and Mexico only, but they do not work for international travel.

Before traveling, be sure to check the expiration date of passports. If they expire in less than six months from the departure date, passengers will not be allowed to fly. These days, many nations including Israel require proof of a fully paid return ticket to the home country before allowing visitors to enter. Singapore was my frightening lesson. I had left my return ticket proof at my temporary base in the Philippines and could have been refused reentry. Thankfully, a Singaporean former student/friend I was visiting was savvy enough on her phone to retrieve my itinerary email that included that information which rescued me.

Carry a photocopy of passports in a safe place in case the original is lost or stolen. I require those traveling with me to give me copies of their passports. I keep those in my trip portfolio along with our complete list of contacts, scheduled stops, reservation confirmations, maps, vital information, and more. That handy, essential portfolio carries my trip "brains" and is usually worn out from use by the time we fly home.

**Visa Requirements**

Today, Israel joins many foreign nations in not requiring entry visas for U.S. or Canadian citizens. The Passport control officers at Israeli Customs grant B2 Entry Permit cards with photo ID to entering U.S., Canadian, and many other visitors. These approve stays of up to ninety days from the arrival date but do not include permission to work.

Those wishing to stay in Israel longer than ninety days must leave the country for any period of time by traveling elsewhere and then reentering. People may visit Turkey, Greece, etc., and then reenter Israel for a fresh visa entitling visitors to a new ninety-day period. (Citizens of other nations can easily learn Israel's requirements online.)

Israel's generally secure and stable borders with Egypt and Jordan permit good travel access. Visas are needed but are easily obtained. However, travelers wishing to visit Bethlehem, the West Bank, or Gaza must pass through Israel Defense Force (IDF) checkpoints. It is recommended that those desiring to visit the last two destinations do so with a tour guide.

Syria and Lebanon do not admit travelers showing proof of having visited Israel. No direct flights connect the countries. The border crossings between Lebanon and Israel at Metula and Rosh HaNikra are jointly supervised by the IDF and UN Interim Forces. Israel's IDF and the United Nations Disengagement Observer Force

(UNDOF) administrate the Quneitra/Kuneitra border area of the demilitarized zone between the Israeli and Syrian sides of the Golan Heights, established by the 1974 UN ceasefire.

There is an excellent overlook approaching the crossing that gives a clear view of the UN Security Forces base. In 2014, we checked with the Army and a local tour guide on the wisdom of traveling past that Quneitra/Kuneitra viewpoint near the UN base overlooking Syria on our day trip to Banias and Mt. Hermon. Damascus is seven miles away. Two miles closer than Damascus, three massive explosions towered into the sky. It looked like we were in our living rooms watching the television evening news— except we suddenly realized we were not. This was real life close at hand, so we hurried on. Later, two planes flew above us. They were painted solid black with no identifying markings, but a retired U.S. Air Force Colonel with us identified them as American. Thankfully, some of the above information is changing.

The Abraham Accord, or Israel-United Arab Emirates normalization agreement, was signed between Israel and the UAE on August 13, 2020. Bahrain also joined, adding their signature to the Accord in Washington D.C. on September 15, 2020. Since then, Sudan has signed and more Arab states are expected to follow. Commercial flights connecting Israel and the United UAE began flying on August 31, 2020. Morocco joined the Accord and established full diplomatic relations with Israel on December 10, 2020. Additional Arab signers are expected.

To simplify travel, Israeli passport control officers no longer stamp the passports of arriving passengers. Instead, they stamp entry on a separate piece of paper kept in the passport until it is collected when visitors depart.

The countries listed below do not yet recognize Israel's existence as a nation so do not allow visitors coming from Israel to travel to them. Check for updates as this situation is changing fairly rapidly.

- Iran
- Iraq

- Afghanistan
- Pakistan
- Lebanon
- Syria
- Kuwait
- Libya

**Health and Medical Tips**

*Vaccination Requirements*

To learn the recommended health and vaccination requirements for Israel or any foreign travel, contact the Centers for Disease Prevention and Control (CDC) via the International Traveler Info Line at 1-877-347-8747. They constantly update their online link https://wwwnc.cdc.gov/travel with current travel advisory guidelines.

In general, Israel is a healthy country with exemplary sanitary conditions. The CDC and WHO (the World Health Organization) do recommend some vaccinations for those visiting Israel. The list contains the same vaccines recommended for citizens living in the U.S. or Canada: Hepatitis A, hepatitis B, typhoid, rabies, anthrax, meningitis, polio, measles, mumps, and rubella (MMR), Tdap (tetanus, diphtheria, and pertussis), chickenpox, shingles, pneumonia, and influenza.

Local medical offices can advise where and when to get vaccinations or immunizations easily and sometimes for free. That information is also available online. Most large universities operate Student Health Services which usually include Travel Clinics open to the public as well as to university students. Plan and phone ahead. The hepatitis B vaccine is a three-dose series on a 0, 1, and 6-month schedule. Recommended doses depend on the person's age and the vaccine brand. The third shot must be at least four months (16 weeks) after the first or at least two months after the second to be fully effective. However, once completed, this vaccination series does not need to be repeated.

*Medical Tips*

Medicare/Medicaid does not typically cover healthcare costs outside of the United States. Check this brochure, "Medical Information for Americans Traveling Abroad" or go to www.CDC.gov

Many travel insurance policies are available for purchase at the price and coverage level that buyers prefer. I have never required medical care overseas, but each time I've phoned my supplemental insurance provider before traveling, they assure me that my coverage includes international care less whatever co-pays apply. However, further investigation makes me suspect there are loopholes in such coverage.

Since I contracted Covid in October 2022 and was traveling to Israel in early January 2023, my concerned older doctor son urged me to buy coverage that could fly me back home if I were ill or deceased. I found a number of excellent policies online that provided much fuller coverage than standard airline trip insurance at little additional cost. In fact, for all of my future travel, instead of standard airline trip insurance, I will only buy the latter. The policy I chose after comparing a number was from Squaremouth.com but there are many out there and conditions may change. By online search, I even found, "Cancel for any reason travel insurance." It's good to know such options exist.

From talking with a North American traveler in Israel who did require care, I learned that her medical bills needed to be paid at the time of treatment, but the charges would be reimbursed once she returned home.

Full information is obtained through a phone call to state or local insurance providers and should bring peace of mind by checking those details in advance. Israel's medical professionals and facilities are considered to be among the world's finest. I hear high praise from those who have received treatment there.

*Medications, Toiletries, First-Aid, Survival Kits, Food, and Drink*

In Israel's hot climate, stay hydrated. When Cindy and I enjoyed field trips with the Biblical Resources staff, they insisted we drink six quarts of water daily. They wouldn't let passengers board the field trip bus without seeing that each of us had brought adequate water. Also bring snacks. Short excursions have a way of lasting longer than expected.

Not all nations have a McDonald's on every corner. Some McDonald's, like the one near Britain's Tower of London housing the Crown Jewels, require people to pay a twenty pence coin to use the restroom, toilet, or loo— even if they are paying restaurant customers. Finally, sunscreen is essential in Israel's intense climate, but most visitors still come home with beautiful golden tans.

Consider the list below and take fewer or more items depending on your personal situation, destinations, weight restrictions, and travel times.

- Antacid
- Antihistamine
- Chapstick (This also works as a great fire starter.)
- Cough drops, cough suppressants, or expectorants
- Decongestant
- Diarrhea medicines (Imodium or Pepto-Bismol)
- Magnifying glass—even a small one can start fires.
- Mild laxative
- Mild sedative or sleep aid
- Motion sickness medicine or patches
- Needles, thread, and snaps and/or buttons
- Pain and fever medicines—acetaminophen (Tylenol), aspirin, or ibuprofen)
- Safety pins of various sizes. These also serve as fishhooks in survival situations.
- String several lengths of strong string or cord can work for fish line or snares.

- Toothpaste
- Vaseline – also rub into chapped skin or dry heels.

*First-aid items to prevent or treat illness or injury*

- 1% hydrocortisone cream
- Aloe gel for sunburns
- Antibacterial or antifungal ointments
- Antiseptic wound cleaner
- Bandages and/or Band-Aids
- Cotton swabs (or Q-Tips)
- Disposable gloves
- Eye drops
- Earplugs
- Gauze
- Hand sanitizer (at least 60% alcohol) or antibacterial hand wipes
- Insect bite anti-itch gel or cream
- Insect repellent (with active ingredients like DEET or picaridin)
- Oral rehydration salts
- Sunscreen (with UVA and UVB protection of SPF 15 or higher)
- Sunglasses and hat
- Thermometer
- Tweezers
- Water purification tablets

Pay attention to signs. At public locations like Ein Gedi, the Dead Sea, and other places, if it says, "Don't drink the water," then "don't drink the water!" During my first visit as an inexperienced traveler, I thought perhaps the sign at Ein Gedi was posted to increase bottled water sales in the gift shop. The water coming from the faucet looked fine but fifteen minutes after drinking a few swallows, I understood their warning. Stomach rumblings made me find my diarrhea meds.

I had not repeated that lapse of judgment since except at Mary's Spring in Ein Kerem on my 2019 visit where the posted sign could only be seen from one side of the flowing spring, and my path approached from the other. I filled my bottle and took several gulps on a hot day before a tourist from the other side ran my way screeching, "Stop! It's contaminated. Throw away your bottle so you don't drink more! Come see the sign!"

She led me to it. I've heard some people have had to be hospitalized.

What does one do when you hear warnings too late? Then, even small stomach rumbles seem like major threats. Thankfully, I remained fine, despite my active imagination.

I've visited nations where we were told to drink bottled water, boil water, or use purification tablets. I'd been warned that restaurants use contaminated water in ice machines in many Asian nations but forgot that in the Philippines once when enjoying an iced mango drink. I suffered the full range of stomach cramps for a week, which fostered weight loss but was inconvenient during travel.

Be smart buying food from street vendors. I believe I have seen fewer of them on streets during recent trips to Israel. Their products may be fine, but buyers take a risk. I got sick once buying a kebab on a Tel Aviv street on a hot day when flies buzzed around. However, with Kosher food laws in place regarding food preparation and many other health details, the food and drink are usually safe! More is said about Kosher foods in Chapter 9's food section. Ice is produced from the general water supply. Tap water in Israel is considered excellent, but most tourists buy bottled water because adjusting to a new supply anywhere can sometimes cause issues.

**Finances, Transportation, and Accommodations**

*Money, Currencies, Banking, Tipping, and VAT Tax*

U.S. and Canadian currencies and credit cards are welcome and easily used. Street vendors accept and appreciate payment in U.S. or Canadian currency. I bring small-denomination bills with me for easy cash purchases. Banks routinely charge fairly steep exchange rates for currency exchange. Israeli Post Offices no longer offer the best rates. ATM machines and foreign exchange locations are readily available in many convenient places. Ask the locals, even passers-by on the street, and they can recommend the best places.

Travelers Checks are not needed. Israel's stable currency unit is the New Israeli Shekel (NIS). Their coins depict ancient biblical images like lilies, the seven-branched candlestick, the lion of Judah, pomegranates, a Phoenician ship, musical instruments, etc.— not the faces of Bible heroes or political leaders. Check the slightly fluctuating Israeli NIS exchange rate online. It usually averages around 3.5 NIS per 1 U.S. dollar or better.

There are a number of ATM stations plus a foreign currency booth at Ben Gurion Airport, but most North American-issued credit cards are accepted well almost anywhere. ATM machines actually often charge less than foreign exchange booths. An older man operating a small booth in Jerusalem's Old City charged me $39 for my transaction instead of the $9 his sign stated. When I inquired, he would not correct the transaction, acting as if he could not understand me. I was frustrated but made no headway—that is the only time something like that has happened to me in Israel or anywhere.

To my joy, my bank back home reversed the extra $30 charge before I asked. Some ATMs routinely post a $5 charge fee for each withdrawal of up to $300 U.S. However, since I've been a good long-term customer at my bank, my local branch voluntarily removed those fees.

On my first few trips to Israel, through my bank I did arrange foreign currency transactions to take the equivalent of $250-$300 U.S. with me in Israeli shekels. The bank charges are steep and the exchange rate not very favorable. Most of us have credit cards that do not charge foreign transaction fees. I usually make sure I carry two of those with me plus some low-denomination U.S. currency bills.

Tipping guidelines compare with North American norms, except you will find people in public service who decline tips, as I occasionally did, because they are grateful to have us visit, support, and enjoy their nation. Few have high incomes but insist it is their pleasure to serve. They may not accept your tip, but it's good to urge them to do so while expressing our appreciation. Whether your servers do accept or not, you will experience their genuine appreciation and feel you have gained new friends.

VAT stands for "Value Added Tax" added to most sales when the item's value is increased by manufacturing raw materials into finished products. The current VAT rate is 17%. Not every shop adds VAT, but many do. Along with saving the receipt when VAT is charged, most merchants will give a VAT certificate if requested. A minimum purchase amount is involved, but the good news is that when leaving Israel's Ben Gurion airport, seaports, or border crossings, you may present your itemized receipts showing VAT charges and request a refund of the extra tax amount. In Ben Gurion, the well-marked VAT refund kiosk is in Terminal 3 and amounts are easily refunded before departure. Add minimal time to stop, but the process does not take long and is worth it.

*Luggage, Duffle Bags, Backpacks, Shipping Charges, Etc.*

Without gruesome details, let's say I've learned the importance of spending money to buy (or borrow) good luggage with free-rolling wheels. Handling a heavy suitcase without wheels when passing through Amsterdam's Schiphol airport, I wrestled my beast onto an escalator between floors instead of lugging it down a long corridor and climbing stairs or finding an elevator. Sadly, part-way down that escalator, gravity tipped my case so I lost hold and it fell backwards, beginning to descend steps. I lunged and grabbed but couldn't catch it.

A man two steps below me lamented in English, "What have I

done to deserve this?" as he lurched to one side but still got sideswiped.

Eventually, my suitcase and I reunited. Soon after, I replaced it with free-rolling wheels so I now painlessly glide along hallways with ease. I also use elevators and avoid escalators.

Judy, one traveler on my 2019 trip, is my all-time hero/heroine for how she coped, although at times she had to use a crutch to support a broken ankle that had almost healed but still needed help and a brace for one arm. I was determined to make the trip manageable for her. Judy was equally determined not to need help. She brought luggage and contents that she could easily manage alone without bothering us. I've never seen anyone pack so well.

Judy brought mix and match clothing pieces rolled up into compact space—enough combinations for two weeks. (We did enjoy the washing machine in our Jerusalem Airbnb). Judy's actual suitcase was 20" x 20" lightweight silver aluminum with wheels and a handle. She also packed treats and powdered beverages to share plus a small well-stocked first-aid kit we benefitted from. I plan to incorporate more of her skills on my future trips.

These days, when so many suitcases are look-alikes, it helps to add identifiable tags, ribbons, bows, cloth strips, or any distinguishing feature to simplify pickup at airport carousels, train platforms, etc.

Travelers can also pack one or more tightly-rolled duffle or zipper bags to bring home extra items to delight family and friends.

Such bags are perfect to fill with clothes or any combination of non-breakable items. At most, people using that method only have to handle and pay extra luggage fees one-way. Usually, it is possible to have purchases like rugs or small furniture items, glassware, dishes, etc., shipped home from most businesses, but be sure to agree on the cost before shipping.

## Transportation Choices

*Plane Flights*

This list is based on my personal experience and is not all-inclusive.

- British Air is one of the best and most reliable carriers and gives excellent service.
- Israel's El Al—I was eager to fly this airline because I had been told that on the way they sang and danced Israeli songs, served Israeli food, and basically introduced passengers to the nation before arrival. Not true. The airline does serve good Israeli food, but their staff was shocked that I'd been told they would sing and dance. However, their pilots fly well and this carrier and its security experts lead the world in travel safety. Business Insider reports, "No flight leaving Ben Gurion has ever been hijacked. El Al, hasn't seen an attack in over 30 years." One effective tool Ben Gurion Airport utilizes to assure excellent security is an automatic security system for checking passengers' luggage is HBS or "Hold Baggage Screening." The system operates by a 100% automatic technological security check method. The system was developed by the Israel Airports Authority to improve service for passengers traveling through Ben Gurion.
- Olympic Air Greece. Generally good carriers, although being on time may not be a priority. I managed to schedule flights with them twice when they've called strikes. The scheduled planes ultimately flew but it was stressful for a while.

*Air Tickets*

Most travelers buy tickets through travel agencies, but there are other options. Usually money is saved and trips are nicely personalized when individuals plan and book their own trips. Consider these tips. The sooner individuals book tickets the better. For international destinations, it's wise to purchase plane tickets around six months in advance for the best deals—and earlier if possible.

After years of travel, I've learned that once the small number of lowest-priced tickets offered is gone, costs rise steadily. When each level of bargain priced seating fills, the price moves up to the next.

When using redeemed air miles for flights, book even earlier. Only a small number of those seats are offered on any flight. As most travelers know, the number of air miles required for trip redemption is at its highest during holidays and peak seasons. Many find the best prices on certain days of the week. So far, I find that to be Tuesdays. Condé Nast also recommends Wednesdays or Saturdays. But it pays to be flexible with dates and take advantage of occasional special sales, etc. Most of us can juggle our travel dates by a day or two in either direction for significant savings. These same guidelines hold true for purchasing rail, ferry, cruise line, bus, or almost any type of travel ticket.

In my early travels, I seldom bought trip insurance and always managed to get myself to airports and onboard flights on the correct day and time. However, today when national disasters and global epidemics affect so much travel worldwide, I do recommend buying trip insurance. Previously, it was possible to make your reservations, think it over a day or two, and then decide if you would buy the insurance. However, almost constantly now, trip protection must be purchased at the time the tickets are booked.

Situations like the Covid variant epidemics are not usually accepted as reasons for trip cancellation and reimbursement. For most other situations, trip insurance is sold at a low enough percentage of the total trip cost to make it a wise investment.

The Covid variant pandemics have taught me new travel lessons. Besides the growing numbers of annual visitors during non-Covid times, Israel has a high number of immigrants making Aliyah, the biblical homecoming of people of Jewish origin returning to the land. This last decade has been Israel's highest rate of return so far, in 2019 receiving over 3,000 immigrants, largely coming from Russia and France. Immigration and citizenship application is based on proven Jewish heritage. It can be denied if Christian involvement is evident.

In March 2011, I had tickets to fly to the Philippines with a plane change and several hours layover in Tokyo's Narita International Airport during Japan's Fukushima Nuclear Disaster. Those of us on the team faced the question of traveling or canceling. Our carrier, Delta Airlines, offered us the option of free cancellation or changing the booking at no cost. I flew anyway and again recognized the geography below.

Instead of flying the normal route down Japan's west coast to Tokyo, on that occasion, the pilot was given permission to enter Soviet Air Space to fly over the Russian Far East, above the Kamchatka Peninsula, and down Japan's east coast to Tokyo to minimize exposure to radiation fallout. It was a beautiful clear flying day. Despite some apprehension, I enjoyed the scenery and got amazing photos. The connecting flights from Tokyo to Manila and back took place without further incident.

*What To Expect When Arriving by Air*

In travel experiences as in relationships, first impressions matter. The nation of Israel does not disappoint. Ben Gurion Airport is the nation's main entry point. Ninety percent of Israel's visitors arrive by air. The remaining ten percent of travelers enter Israel through less-used seaport or land border crossings. Armed soldiers and guards maintain security and monitor entry points well. We feel comfortable and safe seeing armed professionals quietly do their job—not uncomfortable in any way. Other than asking directions, we have never needed to request help, but if necessary, one can generally spot a uniformed police officer or IDF member close by.

I have flown to Ben Gurion on British Air from London Heathrow, on Air Olympus from Athens, KLM from Amsterdam, American Air from Paris, and El Al from Barcelona. British Air and El Al appear to exercise the highest levels of passenger and luggage inspection, but all airlines have stringent security guidelines when Israel is the destination. Most people who experience the demanding pre-boarding screening appreciate the intense scrutiny. I see many reasons to appreciate and none to resent the few extra minutes required.

Tourististrael.com states that Ben Gurion Airport is considered the world's most secure airport. In terms of passenger security, EL AL is one of the world's safest airlines.

For travelers coming from North America, reaching Ben Gurion usually means flying nearly halfway around the world from the time passengers leave their homes and local airports to reach Israel's soil. Few flights take less than 17 hours of travel time. Depending on connecting flights and terminal changes, trips can take up to 30 hours.

A lesser-known transportation option for those traveling to Israel from Greece is to pay passage on or work briefly on a freighter or cruise ship. There may be fewer opportunities during Pandemic times, but it is something to look into. Ferries no longer carry passengers between the countries.

*Transportation Options Inside Israel*

Once you have arrived, this list names the many other means of transport available for seeing the country:

- Bicycles—in many cities and nations, pedal or battery-powered rental bikes are available to be picked up and left off at designated locations.
- Buses
- Cruises
- Ferries
- Hiking and Walking Trails–A famous one is The Jesus Trail in Galilee

- Helicopter and Plane rides can be arranged.
- Hot Air Balloon rides and balloon safaris are available in Israel.

Review the options posted at www.touristisrael.com. My older son and I loved our hot air balloon ride flying over the state borders above Minnesota and Wisconsin offered by Stillwater Balloons. As a grandmother, I found that ride physically manageable, safe, delightful, and the cost was affordable.

Many companies offer good savings through seasonal discount coupons.

- Rail and Light Rail
- RIB (rigid inflatable boats)
- Taxis, Sheruts, and Limousines
- Rental Cars
- Skis, Sleds, Snowboards, Toboggans, Ice Skates, and other winter sports equipment. These are used primarily in Israel's north. A year-round ski resort operates on Mt. Hermon.

On early trips in Israel, my friends and I did lots of walking, rode buses, and occasionally hitchhiked with new friends who were also learning hands-on archaeology, etc.

Taxis are available almost everywhere and it's ideal when several passengers share expenses. Taxis will carry up to four people but cannot always accommodate that much luggage. It generally costs less to find taxis on the street than to phone ahead and re-quest them to pick up passengers because most charge for the travel time to reach you.

For those who don't rent a car at the airport, a good inexpensive pre-order taxi option is Abraham Tours Taxi. Reach them at www.abrahamtours.com once you know flight arrival times to schedule and prepay. Our driver met us by the famous bronze Ben Gurion bust to the right of the airport's main floor exit doors. If flights are delayed, drivers will wait up to 45 minutes but should be tipped accordingly.

In cities like Jerusalem, if you flag down a taxi or find one waiting on the street, I prefer agreeing on the trip price before getting in. I've been pleased with that process and have almost always found pleasant drivers. If they won't agree on a price, I don't go with them. It doesn't take long to find another taxi. Some drivers offer to use a meter for charges, but other travelers have told me horror stories of high rates. Newer Israeli friends do prefer meter use, but I had already found a method that works for me.

If driving in Israel, be aware that the speed limit in Israel is posted in kilometers per hour like Canada, not miles per hour like the U.S. WAZE is a popular, excellent, directional system developed by an Israeli. It and Google Maps both often chart direct routes through the Palestinian territories. Travelers uncomfortable with that routing should check alternate mapping or arrange travel with a guide.

*Drive Yourself?*

By my fourth trip, I realized I could save money and manage time more efficiently if I rented a car to arrange my own travel to be where I wanted to be when. I spent time weighing that option. It sounded challenging but possible. U.S. and Canadian drivers' licenses are recognized in Israel. Foreign visitors do not need an International Driver's License. Israel and the Palestinian territories have clearly identifiable borders and checkpoints.

Israel's major motorways are excellent. Could I stay on recommended roads and not wander into unwise situations? I thought it over, talked with others who had driven there, and gained confidence.

Since my fourth trip, I have rented a vehicle each time and found it a great way for my friends and me to maximize what we want to see and fit more into our schedule while minimizing expenses. By surveying car rental companies online and making reservations far in advance, travelers often score amazing savings. Fuel costs for gasoline and diesel run about twice what they are in the U.S. Check fuel consumption reports when selecting a rental vehicle. Typically, Israeli vehicle sizes are smaller than the majority found in North America. Consider available luggage space when renting a vehicle and when packing.

*Heavy Rail and Light Rail*

Today, train transportation in Israel includes heavy rail (inter-city, commuter, and freight service) as well as light rail. Israel's efficient low-cost light rail system began operation in 2011 and is an excellent travel option. In Jerusalem its first stage initially only ran up and down Jaffa Street. Expansions since have connected it to neighborhoods further away from the city and added increasingly distant points, even now servicing Ben Gurion Airport and Tel Aviv.

My light rail error on a recent trip came from assuming that the Jaffa Street light rail still only traveled up and down Jaffa Street while expansion actually took it further. I had visited Jerusalem during the light rail's early construction stage, often encountering the deep open gash intersecting the city's thoroughfares and complicating traffic.

Back in Jerusalem again, I confidently bought tickets at the automated kiosks positioned along the route and waved my friends on board. However, instead of taking us to our destination at the Clal Center, one of the city's tallest office towers and indoor shopping malls at 97 Jaffa Rd., the train sped to a new area that made my friends and me have to walk quite a distance. I learned a lesson, apologized profusely, and will not repeat that mistake.

It's never fun being lost. Whether you're an iPhone or GPS fan, or rely on city or national maps provided by some businesses, reliable maps or electronic direction-finding apps are crucial. Sometimes, I've received excellent maps and brochures at no cost by contacting U.S. branches of Israel's Tourism Bureau online at GoIsrael.com.

Earth's twenty-four time zones mean that crossing the International Dateline going east or west adds or subtracts a full day depending on the direction traveled. Flying west, travelers sometimes reach destination airports earlier than the time they left their departure city! From where I'm writing in the U.S. Central Time Zone, London is six hours ahead of us, most of mainland Europe is seven hours, and Israel is eight hours later than the Central U.S.

Read the fine print. Air, bus, and train schedules use 24-hour schedules. Booking train tickets online costs about half the price of buying them at stations. By mistake once in Italy, I bought tickets for a train leaving Venice at 8 a.m., twelve hours before my friends and my intended 8 p.m. departure.

Thankfully, the conductor accepted the tickets and didn't put us off in the middle of nowhere as he did the passenger with no ticket at all. However, he could not provide us seats. We had to stand or sit on the train floor in corridor space near the car's entrance the whole way, but we appreciated the ride.

### Rental Cars

Rental car agencies wish to please clients. The best availability and rates are found far in advance. Some companies require pre-paid bookings, but if there is a need to cancel up to 24-hours before the reservation date, a full refund is usually given. The exception is that following the Covid and variant pandemic, some hard-hit agencies gave vouchers good for one or two years instead. Many emails and persevering phone calls usually resolved that problem.

When a large-size or handicapped equipped vehicle is needed, that's all the more reason to make reservations early. For requests beyond the ordinary, rental agencies typically send a message confirming tentative confirmation but then reconfirming close to the actual travel date with details on the exact vehicle they will provide.

So far, I have been pleased with rentals, although some agencies added surprise charges that were not discussed initially. Last time, the agency I used substituted a different make and model than the van requested, but the replacement had more passenger space and better gas mileage. I will happily use them again.

Rental car returns—when returning car rentals at Ben Gurion

Airport, be aware that despite the orange signs directing drivers to the rental return lots, they are still hard to find, especially at 2-3 a.m. for 5-6 a.m. departures, true for many trans-Atlantic flights.

Also, not all rental cars are to be brought to Departures Terminal 3. One agency offers a $35 price break if the car is returned to Arrivals Terminal 1 instead. Allow extra time for completing rental paperwork and the shuttle ride to the main terminal for Departures. When returning a car during nighttime hours, it can be hard to get a printed receipt. Some agencies wave a hand and say, "We'll email it to you." That has not worked well for me and there were charges that needed challenging. If at all possible, get a printed receipt when you turn the car in.

I once led a group of fifteen people by hiring a bus and driver through a joint U.S.-Israeli travel agency. Another time, I led eight people riding in two cars, and once six people in one Korean-made nine-passenger van. (The latter size is hard to find in Israel these days. Some say that the current unavailability of large vans is to encourage tourists to hire local guides with their own vehicles instead). Of the arrangements I've used, I recommend carrying four to six passengers in one vehicle for the best and most easily managed travel experience.

After arriving in Israel and picking up a rental car, be aware that when exiting the airport to drive to Tel Aviv or Jerusalem, all cars pass through a toll gate where drivers receive a machine-generated ticket. This concerned me my first few trips as I didn't want to receive a running toll charge. However, the automated ticket is a routine part of leaving the airport and no toll charges have been added to our rental contracts.

*Accessibility–the Disabled May Travel, Too*

Throughout Israel, travel is also possible for most people with temporary or permanent disabilities. Physical restrictions do not need to limit most travelers. While attending a writing seminar on a cruise ship, I met an older gentleman who expressed sorrow that he had not visited Israel when he was young and fit. Discouraged by the limitations that can accompany aging, he felt overwhelmed by the idea of buying and shipping the motorized scooter he thought he would need. He still appeared healthy and strong but did use a scooter with him to cover distances on the cruise ship and in ports.

I was happy to tell him that nothing need delay his trip to Israel. Just as tourists rent cars for visits there, it's very possible to rent reliable equipment. In a short time online, I found many options for motorized wheelchairs, mobility scooters, and many other helps to simplify travel for around the same price people pay in North America.

Instead of taking a motorized wheelchair, travelers should plan to rent one where they're going. If they are unsure of their ability to navigate in a strange setting upon arrival, the ideal equipment can almost always be rented at the destination.

Before a trip to Denmark to see a student who had lived a year in our home, I'd torn a meniscus that required emergency knee surgery. When I booked my flight, I requested an aisle because of that limitation, and Iceland Air gave me an aisle seat in a better section of the plane for no extra cost plus a wheelchair at my destination to take me to my friends in the airport.

These days, battery-powered scooters and bicycles are great options, and some are lightweight, foldable, and portable. It appears that the same laws covering scooter use apply to electric bicycles. In most centers, they may be ridden on paths, trails, and on streets with bike lanes. No license, registration, or insurance is required, but sidewalks are off-limits.

Popular two-wheeled upright Segway rentals are another consideration. Traveladvisor.com offers a two-hour Segway Tour of Old Jerusalem. I'm looking forward to receiving a postcard from the cruise ship gentleman saying he has taken and enjoyed his trip.

For those with serious limitations, cruise ships offer reasonably priced fully handicapped-accessible suites. A friend restricted to a motorized wheelchair was very pleased with this option. His brother traveled with him, and a cruise line attendant helped at set times with bed to chair transfers, etc. The suite contained a generously sized roll-in shower with a Hoyer Hoist and other accessories. This was provided at what my friend considered little additional cost beyond standard per person fare. He intends to go again.

The level of support services may differ between cruise lines, but many offer handicapped suites. Reports say that disabled passengers enjoy bigger suite spaces and more services for amazingly little additional price. If this is an option travelers wish to consider, rates and information are easily found online.

On my 2019 trip to Israel, we visited a favorite resort on the Sea of Galilee when several buses of cruise ship passengers arrived as part of their add-on land tour. At least one wheelchair-restricted person remained on the bus during that stop but was cared for well and her meal served to her there.

On that same trip, one friend had suffered a repeated ankle fracture eight weeks prior to our departure. Judy fills many public roles, including teaching classes on Israel and the Bible so had long desired to visit. Determined to take the trip despite injuries, she obtained her doctor's release and used a crutch and brace as needed, which sometimes compromised her shoulder. My earlier stays in Israel had taught me where to find rare public parking lots and when it was smarter to hire a cab and share costs instead of driving ourselves.

For example, our rented condo was .7 miles from The Garden Tomb. We decided to walk there (mostly downhill) but take a cab home. Judy didn't want to miss anything. So, with the best attitude in the world, that day she walked four miles with us along the Via Dolorosa to the Church of Saint Anne with its magnificent alabaster ceiling that may have the best musical acoustics this side of heaven. It is constructed over a grotto that Crusaders believed was the childhood home of Mary, the mother of Jesus.

Judy could not manage the steep steps leading down to the Pool of Bethesda, but I took enough photos for all of us. She was thrilled with what she accomplished and slept soundly that night. I am happy to say she has since fully recovered and is happy that she managed every part of our trip.

The streets of Old City Jerusalem are ancient cobblestones with ramps along one side maybe one foot long or less that accommodate bicycles, wheelbarrows, and even wheelchairs to descend the steps. Important routes like the Via Dolorosa would be bumpy and a bit difficult to navigate by wheelchair, but not impossible. I saw several people doing so.

In other words, there is little reason to prevent almost anyone from traveling freely throughout Israel. Most solutions that enable people to travel successfully in North America are available there. Online, I easily found a number of Israeli disability equipment providers. Arrangements simply need to be made in advance. If needed, it should also be possible to rent or hire a handicapped van. Travel is possible for most situations and destinations where people wish to go. That includes cruise ship tours that travel the Mediterranean and offer add-on land excursions in Israel.

Similar to Handicapped parking spaces in North America, Israel designates many convenient parking spots near to destinations. Handicapped permits from other nations are honored in Israel. If travelers have a permit, bring it. If it is forgotten, have someone back home take a photo and email it. When printed, simply display that copy on the car dash. We followed those steps on our last trip and it added great convenience when our teammate, Judy, needed and deserved that consideration.

Before her emailed Handicapped permit had arrived, I parked in a handicapped space when a taxi driver came up behind me and honked impatiently for me to leave. I rolled down my car window, I waved my friend's crutch outside for him to see, and he left.

## Accommodation Options

*Airbnb Rentals, Hotels, Hostels, Kibbutzes, Moshavs, Etc.*

On that first trip, Cindy and I did not have the funds to stay thirty-six days in Israeli hotels but also desired to be more than typical tourists. We preferred maximum interaction with the nation's people. During my year of planning, I investigated hotels, hostels, room rentals, bed and breakfasts, and many other options.

It's good to be aware that fewer buildings in Israel have elevators than we're used to in North America. Requesting main-floor rooms when making reservations is no guarantee that you will get them. If that is a need for you and your team, personally check with the accommodation manager before arriving, not a booking company that may have been a go-between.

Israel values energy independence. The nation's hot water is supplied through the efficient white solar water heaters dotting rooftops everywhere. That means that as days heat up, there is plenty of hot water through the evenings, but morning showers can be cool unless supplemental electricity is used to heat water before the sun is up and hot. Plan accordingly. These days, most tourist facility hosts will use enough additional electricity to insure their guests' comfort. On one trip my group of eight encountered an exception in Tiberias, though, and the last person to line up for a shower each day only found cold.

For our January 2023 trip, an online search let me hit the jackpot in the Lower Galilee. Instead of staying in Tiberias, I looked for a country setting. It didn't have to provide Sea of Galilee waterfront, but needed to be comfortable and affordable. We stayed three nights in The Shavit Family Guest Houses in the small farming community of Arbel with views of Tiberias 4.2 miles away.

The property had many trees with the ripest, sweetest oranges I've ever eaten along with grapefruit, tangerines, persimmons, grapes, and more. We were told to eat all we could and take lots with us. We'd go there again in a heartbeat.

*Hotels*

Hotels throughout Israel are very similar to those in North

America, so it is easy to research their options online. The same five-star rating scale applies as well. Most offer frequent-stay discount programs worth enrolling in for guests staying more than one night, even if you don't plan to return. Therefore, the added information below focuses primarily on accommodation options other than hotels.

*Airbnb*

Airbnb rental homes away from home didn't exist when I first began traveling in Israel. Today, they are numerous and popular with most offering fairly nice places at attractive prices. However, one of my teams was disappointed with the large flat we rented in Tiberias that accommodated eight of us well but could only be accessed by driving the wrong way up a steep one-way street. Building residents said they all reached the building the same way. Our unit was on the third floor with narrow steps and no elevator.

That's also the hot water supply that consistently failed, but the view of the Sea of Galilee was glorious. We made memories, and appreciated our low shared cost, but will not stay there again. To avoid disappointments, I now more carefully check reviews from other guests who have stayed in the rentals or request references. Our Airbnb finds since then have been great.

While preparing for my first trip to Israel, I had written to Wycliffe Bible Translators, Youth with a Mission, Open Doors, and numerous Christian organizations. My letter to Christ for the Nations Institute in Dallas, Texas, brought the best results. They forwarded my inquiry to an affiliated organization, Christian Friends of Israel, in Jerusalem. That director connected me with Tina and Moshe Goldenberg, a fascinating couple, who offered bed and breakfast space in their home. Moshe was completing his doctoral degree in advanced molecular particle physics at Hebrew University. Tina organized used clothing for Holocaust survivors as well as volunteered with other Jerusalem Christian organizations.

Moshe's letter instructed us to ride from the airport in one of the sheruts then available there. Those were large eight to ten passenger sedans or minivans that strangers hired and shared to reach their destinations. After an hour's ride, Cindy and I were the last passengers to be dropped off. The Goldenbergs lived in an apartment complex in Gilo, in the valley of Rephaim, on the southwestern edge of Jerusalem four miles north of Bethlehem where David, the shepherd boy, killed Goliath. Moshe said to have the driver phone him on arrival and he would bring the correct payment in shekels.

Moshe's dark hair and curly beard enhanced his studious thoughtful personality. At his side, Tina was a lively blue-eyed blonde Dutch woman nineteen years his senior, but they are great together, showing few signs of age difference. She had been a missionary nurse to Brazil for six years before returning to the Netherlands. She later made thirty hair-raising Bible smuggling trips into Eastern European countries for Brother Andrew's Open Doors organization. While visiting friends in Israel, she met Moshe, a Jewish believer. The rest is history.

During my year of preparation before traveling to Israel, my research and inquiries pulled much of our travel puzzle together. However, meeting Moshe and Tina filled in the remaining missing pieces. Not only did we form a warm lasting friendship, but they introduced us to hostels, fellowship groups, and amazing families and individuals throughout Israel. Nearly forty years later, I stay in close touch with them and others as well.

### Hostels

Little known in North America, but much more common throughout Europe, Israel has many secular and Christian low-cost hostels in major cities like Joppa, Tel Aviv, Jerusalem, Haifa, Tiberias, Dead Sea areas, Eilat, Beersheba, and other places. One reason I'm a fan of hostels is for their opportunities to interact with a wide spectrum of other guests.

Hostels are inexpensive shared accommodations that years ago were basic dormitory style with a kitchen and common area. I once stayed in one in Amsterdam where guests were advised to sleep with their passport and valuables in the pillowcase under their head. Thankfully, I haven't heard that warning since. However, it is important to be wise in safeguarding valuables.

While on our way to Israel on that first trip, Cindy and I spent one night at another place in Amsterdam. There were no rooms left in the recommended Christian hostel, so we booked the last two beds in a four-bed room in a nearby secular hostel. To our surprise, instead of sharing that room with "Carol and Michelle" from Canada, we found ourselves with "Carol and Michael," but all behaved well and we were fine.

Hostels have improved through the years. Most now offer private rooms that accommodate two, three, four, or even six or more people. Most include private bathrooms. If not, well-maintained restrooms are in hallways nearby.

Since my first trip to Israel in 1984, I have enjoyed staying in many hostels throughout the country. I consider them windows into Israel's life and soul that also provide great networking and fellowship opportunities.

I am comfortable in secular or Christian facilities. Abraham's Hostels are a popular secular choice in Tel Aviv and Jerusalem and other world centers with adequate rooms, good food, and pleasant staff. However, if travelers are driving, finding available, affordable parking in Tel Aviv or Jerusalem is very difficult. Interestingly, Dublin, Ireland also has an Abraham's Hostel that has been voted, "the best value hostel" in that city.

If you rent a vehicle but lack parking arrangements, it adds extreme pressure to your travels. We learned one lesson the hard way. We found a parking space in Jaffa that was almost too good to be true (because it was). No part of a parked vehicle may touch or cover any part of a crosswalk. The charge for that offense is 250 NIS or over $73 U.S. plus another $22 U.S. to transfer the ticket from the rental car company's name to the renter's name and passport number. Fines are higher for other offenses like nosing into a bus lane for mere seconds while turning a car around but being caught on camera. (Don't ask how we know.)

I especially love how hostels provide opportunities to meet and interact with people from everywhere around the world. It's incredible. Almost every time, while meeting guests from other nations, I discover at least one with whom I share mutual friends.

Even for travelers unaccustomed to sharing accommodation with strangers, most hostels now offer private sleeping rooms and often with a private bathroom included. Everyone on my teams who has

spent time in hostels has loved the experience, even if it was not something they had done previously. They also felt it helped them connect genuinely with the country.

This online site https://www.cmj-israel.org/christ-church-guest-house features three excellent Christian hostels in great locations: Beit Immanuel near Old Jaffa in Tel Aviv, Beit Bracha in Migdal (near Tiberias) on the Sea of Galilee, and Christ Church Guest House inside Jaffa Gate in Old City, Jerusalem. These all provide generous Israeli breakfasts with delicious breads, cereals, eggs, vegetables, cheeses, fruits, sometimes meats, and beverages. Other meals can usually be arranged by registering in advance.

Christ Church, the oldest Protestant Church in the Middle East, has a small but good free museum plus a good coffee shop we use as a trip base for our team members to meet and rest if they are weary or to reconnect if we get separated. Staff volunteers have become friends we look forward to seeing on each visit.

*Kibbutzes* (or *Kibbutzim*, the plural in Hebrew)

Another popular, affordable accommodation choice is to lodge in one of Israel's many kibbutzes. Staying even one or two nights gives delightful authentic insights into Israeli life. It reveals much of the spirit and history of the nation during its modern settlement period and growth into statehood.

Kibbutz means "gathering or clustering." These agricultural collective communities are unique to Israel. Their members are called Kibbutzniks. The earliest communities were founded before Israel became a nation by desperate Eastern European Jewish refugees with determination but little farming background. They grew from the need to survive and sustain themselves more than from social or political idealism. When several early ones floundered, they received support from European Jewish philanthropists like Barons De Hirsch, Rothschild, and others. From around 1905, the refugees arriving were indoctrinated with Zionism and a determination to redeem malarial swampy ground into productive land. Most of those flourishing today were established in the 1920s. Today, there are over 270. Most have diversified beyond agriculture and are now privatized.

Located where the Jordan River flows south from the Sea of Galilee, Degania Alef, was the first kibbutz founded by Eastern European pioneers. Featured in Leon Uris's book and movie, *Exodus*, unproductive swamp land was bought. To drain the land, twenty hardworking young men and women dug countless ditches and planted Australian Eucalyptus trees to absorb malarial water. An irrigation ditch system was created to carry good water. Field work was done under the protection of armed guards because local Arabs and Bedouins were not pleased with newcomers buying and working even worthless land.

Take time to tour the area. Visit their small excellent museum. We enjoyed shopping in their general store. Some kibbutzes also have thrift or specialty craft stores open to the public.

Most kibbutzes welcome visitors for basic but comfortable overnight stays and meals at reasonable cost. Many also offer work-stay opportunities. Volunteering programs encourage people aged 18 to 35 especially, but inquiries may be made for all age groups.

My favorite kibbutz experience is Kalia Guest House whose managers also operate Israel's biggest date plantation and Kalia Beach Resort on the Dead Sea with excellent bathing, restaurants, gift shops, and camel rides.

Immediately to its south, the kibbutz also manages the famous high-traffic Qumran Touring Center in Qumran National Park.

That includes a large busy restaurant, well-stocked gift shops, and a visitor Center with audio-visual presentations on the Essenes and the Dead Sea Scrolls. Visitors may tour the Essene settlement remains and hike close to the cave where the Dead Sea Scrolls were found.

Overnight stays at Kalia Guest Houses entitle guests to outstanding breakfasts in the kibbutz dining room plus free admission and towels for the very nice Kalia Beach Resort on the Dead Sea. A young husband and father at Kalia kindly drove us from the dining room to the ceramic studio on his golf cart and described meeting and marrying his wife in Tel Aviv. Although his wife had grown up on a kibbutz, they had not planned to live on one. But a year into marriage, his wife said, "All I want is to raise our family next door to my mother on the kibbutz."

Unconvinced, he came for a visit fifteen years ago. Now with four children, this husband and father smiled broadly saying, "We're happy. It's the best decision we ever made."

*Moshavs*

Moshavs are another type of Israeli cooperative settlement, but instead of having collective ownership like a kibbutz, land parcels here are owned individually by members who choose the benefits of voluntarily living and working together. In their beginnings, these were primarily agricultural, but many have now diversified into industrial production. Most also offer guest accommodations.

Because I had a full year to research possibilities before my first trip to Israel, most pieces of our travel puzzle were in place. As mentioned, Cindy and I stayed with Tina and Moshe Goldenberg and formed a lasting friendship. They in turn put us in touch with Christian and secular hostels and connected us with families and fellowship groups throughout Israel. After nearly forty years, it's wonderful to still keep in touch and stay current with genuine Israeli families regarding their lives and national situations.

*Summary*

I cannot provide an exact ranking but in my experience hotels are the most expensive places to stay and the least authentic in displaying everyday life in Israel. Israeli hotels are similar to those almost anywhere in the world. Some in Israel provide continental or full breakfasts or may offer that for an additional charge. It is important to check to see if parking is available and if there is an additional cost.

Hostels typically cost less than hotels and almost always include generous breakfasts in a community dining room and usually with other amenities besides. Free parking is usually included.

Airbnbs can be rented for costs ranging from low to high depending on the location and amenities desired. These usually include kitchen space to manage your own meals if you wish, as well as laundry facilities. Parking is often available but don't take that for granted. Sometimes, there is a charge. Our 2023 trip showed me how extremely essential parking arrangements are. I personally recommend the accommodation options below.

**Abraham Hostels** in Jerusalem and Tel Aviv, www.abrahamhostels.com

**Beit Immanuel**, 8 Auerbach St., Joppa (Tel Aviv), https://www.cmj-israel.org/beit-immanuel

**Jerusalem YMCA Three Arches Hotel**, 26 King David Street, Jerusalem, 91002 (great location) https://www.booking.com/hotel/il/ymca.html

**The King David Hotel** is expensive but worth seeing. Check out their fancy restrooms. Even buying a cup of coffee is a costly but interesting experience. Part of the movie *Exodus* was filmed there.

**Christ Church (Anglican) Guest House**, Coffee House, good small museum, and more—Just past the Post Office inside Jaffa Gate in Old City, Jerusalem, Christ Church is the oldest Protestant church in the Middle East.

**The Dan Hotels** in Tel Aviv and Jerusalem are a fair-priced hotel chain with multiple good locations and prices–www.danhotels.com

**The Shelter Hostel**, Eilat, https://www.shelterhostel.com/en/

**Volunteer and Educational Opportunities**

Visitors to Israel may also consider short or long-term volunteer or educational opportunities. Some colleges and universities offering English-language courses and degrees include Ariel University, Bar Ilan University, Ben-Gurion University, University of Haifa, Hebrew University, Tel Aviv University, Technion Israel–Institute of Technology, Weizmann Institute of Science, IDC Herzliya, Machon Lev/Machon Tal with Israel's leading nursing program, and more.

For a list of Israel's short- to long-term programs in English leading to Bachelor's and Master's degrees, see University Programs in English: Studying in Israel | Nefesh B'Nefesh.

Barring delays due to things like Covid variant outbreaks, the nation's Council for Higher Education intended to double the number of international students to 24,000 by the end of 2022 and has approved twenty-six new English-language degree programs. Learn more at https://www.israel21c.org/26-new-english-language-degree-programs-approved-in-israel

Another great option for travelers to spend time in Israel is giving volunteer service in exchange for meals and places to stay at many guest houses, hostels, and kibbutzes, or other perks. Those interested should inquire directly to the locations they prefer and ask about requirements and allowable lengths of stay. On my first trip to Israel, Cindy and I met a staff person at Biblical Resources Training Center, now relocated to LaGrange, Georgia, USA. We enjoyed volunteering with them, which meant they included us in training lectures and several trips. I still use the valuable notes received from them.

**Volunteering Categories**

- Marine Conservation
- Desert Wildlife Conservation
- EcoBuilding

- Teaching English to At-Risk Youth
- Archaeology dig teams
- Helping in vineyards
- Volunteering in bakeries

Additional volunteer opportunities are easily found online. Opportunities exist for volunteers to participate on Archaeology dig teams. Yearly, the February issue of *Bible Archaeology Review* (BAR) publishes a list of active dig sites that accept volunteers who pay low board and room fees and usually receive college credit. The magazine's publisher, the Biblical Archaeology Society, offers $2,000 dig scholarships to those wishing to participate who demonstrate financial need. I highly recommend volunteer dig experiences. Important finds are sometimes discovered by amateurs, although the artifacts remain the property of the nation's Israel Antiquities Authority. Learn more at https://mfa.gov.il/MFA/IsraelExperience/History/Pages/Archaeological-Excavations-in-Israel-2020.aspx

Also investigate participating at Emek Tzurim National Park located on the lower western slope of the Mount of Olives and Mount Scopus and the upper reaches of the Kidron Valley. It is accessible by city bus. Volunteers sift materials excavated at the City of David.

On our first trip to Israel, Cindy and I worked several days as volunteers at a then active site in the Valley of Rephaim, the valley of the giants between Gilo and Bethlehem. Sixth-century BC/BCE Canaanite homes were being uncovered and revealed a beautiful mosaic floor along with a wealth of pottery shards. I spent one afternoon working alongside the dig's pottery expert learning to re-assemble broken shards by matching the pottery's color, material, texture, location found, and vessel shape. I loved that experience.

New information was recently uncovered at the Horvat Hani (Khirbet el-Burj el-Haniyeh) site taking its importance further back than was previously known. It may have been the burial place of Hannah, mother of the prophet Samuel. See www.Medievalists.net/2022/08/medieval-convent-restored-in-israel-after-being-accidentally-damaged.

Early British Archaeologist, Flinders Petrie, established a reliable dating system based on the types and shapes of pottery pieces found. Such projects are like being involved in the world's most fascinating jigsaw puzzles.

Until the air-conditioned bombproof Israeli Museum was built to house and safeguard the Dead Sea Scrolls, Israel's Antiquities Authority worked on them in East Jerusalem's Rockefeller Museum. Discovered in 1946, two years before Israel's birth as a nation, many consider the scrolls to be a property deed confirming Jewish scriptures and ownership of the land.

Many travelers create Dream List Destinations—everything from glamorous luxury tent camping (or "glamping") in Petra, Jordan, to unique stays at a Negev Camel Ranch, a working farm near Dimona, Israel, where guests can take camel-back excursions into the Negev Desert for periods ranging from one hour to up to two days. We enjoyed our stay there in 2023. I believe they can accommodate people with disabilities, but that and other destination answers are easily learned online.

Tourism is one of Israel's greatest income sources and except during the Covid variant pandemics, those numbers have steadily risen. They warmly welcome and take excellent care of visitors. In 2017, a record 3.6 million tourists arrived from all over the world, a 25 percent increase from 2016, adding NIS 20 billion to the economy (an all-time high worth nearly 6 billion U.S. dollars). Despite occasional terrorist events, increasing tourism is proof of travelers' confidence in Israel's IDF and security forces.

Jerusalem's Old City is divided into four distinct quarters.

From the northern 12 o'clock position moving clockwise, they are Muslim, Jewish, Armenian, and Christian. They are inside 40' tall, crenellated walls built by Suleiman I, the Magnificent, Sultan of the Ottoman Empire, before his death in 1566 AD/CE. The strong, chariot-wide walls have served as effective military fortifications ever since. The full perimeter is easily traveled as the Ramparts Walk, an easy walking route for visitors to enjoy. From its elevated view, all of the Old City is easily seen as well as its neighborhoods beyond. The admission price is low and the experience worthwhile. The walk may be completed in a single day or spread over several days as people wish.

On a recent trip, our group of eight stopped in the Armenian Quarter while I asked a local gentleman standing by an arch to confirm we were on the correct narrow cobblestone street to reach our destination. That Quarter specializes in beautiful hand-painted ceramics. We were on track, but in conversation he mentioned being able to access local sites that are usually off limits to the public.

His kids attend U.S. colleges. He lives in Minnesota for half of the year and named people and places I knew and showed us his Minnesota driver's license. He resides in the Armenian Quarter the other six months and his connections allowed him to get us inside a locked churchyard and see ruins dating to the fourth century AD/CE, plus more if we were interested. We were. We enjoyed places we would not have seen otherwise. Friendly and likable, he pointed out that his time was worth something. We each gave him around $10 U.S.

On our first trip to Israel when Tina couldn't accompany us, or Cindy and I forgot her lessons, we used trial and error to find which Old City quarters were welcoming and where it was safest to shop. That trip took place during the first Intifada, a Palestinian uprising against Israeli presence in the West Bank and Gaza. With tensions high, most shoppers avoided Arab businesses. Without realizing it, Cindy and I crossed some invisible line because when we barely stepped inside the doorway of one shop, its proprietor quickly pulled down the folding metal security grill from above his entrance and locked us in.

"The Intifada is bad," he said frowning fiercely. "I will release you when you buy enough to feed my family."

"But we—"

He looked desperate, not threatening. Thankfully, Cindy and I had followed Tina's counsel and dressed modestly (which was our usual practice anyway).

"We're poor travelers from Canada," I said. "We don't have much money, but will buy a few things." I chose two small carved olive wood camels. Cindy selected jewelry.

The shopkeeper warmed. "Now we are friends. Shop more while I fix you something to drink. Turkish coffee? Or hot sweet tea?"

"Coffee for me, please," I said predictably. Cindy requested tea. He lifted her hand and kissed it before hurrying to a curtained corner to light his kettle.

Cindy paled. "He has six fingers!!!"

Yes, I'd noticed also—six fingers like the Bible describes Goliath and his family of giants who had lived just a few miles away. "He has six toes, too," I said.

We drank his delicious beverages. The tea was fragrant with cardamom. My sweet thick Turkish coffee was delicious. The shopkeeper discussed life and hardships in our countries. After we paid for our purchases, he unlocked and raised his steel gate. As we re-entered the ancient narrow cobblestone street to retrace our steps, other merchants gathered. Our new friend explained that we had bought from him but were poor, nice Canadians—not rich Americans.

The merchants shared their plights. They all had hungry children at home. Politics high above them defined their lives. They felt helpless in an ancient ongoing conflict. They knew there was little we could do, but it helped that we listened. Within minutes, the mood calmed, and they let us leave. I paid closer attention to Old City areas after that, thankful that our incident ended peacefully but wiser for the experience.

Male and female well-armed Israeli Defense Force soldiers appeared everywhere, even in pill box sniper nests on rooftops near the Western Wall. One day, I got bug-eyed watching a strong young Israeli girl soldier stride past us into a nearby alley with two Uzis crisscrossed across her back. I started to follow to snap a photo until I realized she might not like being pursued down an alley and could question my motive. I lowered my camera and turned around.

Seeing soldiers present everywhere made us feel protected, not endangered. Most were pleasant, welcoming, and quick to help when we asked for directions. One shared foil-wrapped heartshaped chocolates with us, thanking us for coming as friends to his land.

Tina warned us to avoid questionable areas at night—especially Silwan (biblical Siloam) with Hezekiah's Water Tunnel where hostility often took place. In fact, we were told world TV cameras were trained on that area 24/7 to capture news.

That next Sunday morning, Cindy and I attended Narkiss Street Baptist Church. Their choir sang a lovely song I had not heard before based on Psalm 34, "The angel of the Lord encamps 'round those who fear His Name to save them and deliver them from harm..."

After church, we headed toward the Mount of Olives. I unfolded my map and found a shortcut leading from our location through the Dung Gate and the Valley of Hinnom or Gehenna where some of Judah's kings had sacrificed their children to Moloch by fire.

Either I forgot part of that terrible history or suffered temporary insanity because I only based our route on the shortest distance between two points—not history or politics.

The day was hot. As we walked, the road dipped down from the Old City into a desolate forsaken area. Judas had hung himself there after betraying Jesus to evil men to force the Lord to declare his kingdom.

We saw caves on the valley's southern side, but I concentrated on the buildings and signs of civilization I saw ahead in Silwan in the distance. Meanwhile, Cindy noticed an agitated man approaching fast from a cave to the right and asked me, "Do you fear the Lord?"

"Yes," I answered and then looked where she pointed. Dressed in a long black robe with a turban wound around his head, a sinister-looking stranger advanced toward us. We needed an angel of the Lord!

As thoughts raced through my mind, the man kept coming closer. Just before he reached us, we heard a noisy clatter behind and turned to see a bright yellow cab roaring in our direction stuffed with passengers hanging out of its open windows. Leaving the Old City behind, it sped along this desolate stretch leading to Silwan on the Mount of Olives' lower slopes.

When the man saw the taxi, he stopped, turned, and whistled several distinct notes to someone in the caves we could not see. The man quickly retraced his steps as the cab stayed in sight while driving the long open stretch to Silwan. Cindy and I walked forward fast and soon spotted a line of sandbags dividing the road where houses began.

"Road construction," my practical North American mind told me. Wrong. This was the dividing line between East and West Jerusalem. An Israeli police or IDF jeep was parked in front of the next two-story home. Four armed men in uniform climbed that home's steps and ushered out men with their hands in the air.

Tippy toe, tippy toe, we slowly inched forward, trying to be invisible. We had barely passed the jeep when shots rang out. I literally looked down at my chest to see if I was bleeding. I was not. Just then an eight or nine-year old boy ran to us and grabbed my arm.

"Come quickly into my father's shop." I stared. "What?"

"Don't you feel it? Quickly, before the tear gas gets you."

We let him steer us through the cool dark entryway of a modest shop. Minutes passed and occasionally people entered paying money for candles. We bought a few small items and when things calmed, stood to leave. "Wait," the boy said. "Don't you want to come all the way inside?"

"Inside where?" I asked. "Hezekiah's Water Tunnel!"

We had not intended to ignore Tina's warnings. We'd reached that destination by accident but did not enter the tunnel. Hopefully, intentions count for something! I paid closer attention to her instructions after that. We saved going to the Mount of Olives for another day and returned to Gilo instead. We confessed and Tina forgave us, especially since our error wasn't intentional.

"I'm glad you're here instead of on the evening news," she said.

We had much to learn, and I began compiling a survivor's journal.

The point is, it's important to be careful when visiting anywhere. We were accidentally in an area where we shouldn't have been.

The main purpose of my early trips to Israel was to study and absorb all I could to give effective teachings on Biblical Archaeology and later on the History of Ancient Israel. However, the more I learned, the more I realized I wanted to learn for my own enjoyment as well, so we volunteered at recommended institutes to hear experts that added to our storehouses of knowledge.

One organization then was Biblical Resources Training Center and Scripture Garden led by archaeologist, Dr. Jim Fleming, then based at Tantur between Gilo and Bethlehem. Cindy and I did odd jobs like painting benches and organizing files in exchange for sitting in on lectures and receiving excellent teaching materials I still use. They also took us along on two great field trips. That organization has since relocated to La Grange, Georgia, still under Dr. Fleming's leadership but is renamed the Biblical Resources Center with displays including artifacts released to them by the Israeli Antiquities Authority.

I encourage travelers to consider the many available volunteering opportunities in Israel. The hands-on benefits received almost always outweigh the actual work done, plus provide great learning opportunities and fostering new relationships.

**Main Travel Choices After Landing in Tel Aviv**

On my first three trips to Israel, I did what most tourists do— traveled from Ben Gurion Airport straight to Jerusalem. As years passed, I realized that if I wished to trace the life of Jesus historically and chronologically, I would start in Galilee instead. That's when I first rented a car to arrange my own travels.

My first trip involved lots of bus rides. I didn't recognize that Jewish and Arab buses were different. Cindy and I boarded a bus in Haifa whose destination sign said Tiberias without noticing it was an Arab bus that stopped in Nazareth. We were the only western women on board. In fact, we were the only women. I sat next to an elderly sheikh dressed in robes. He slept most of the way. It was hot. Sitting one row ahead of me next to another passenger, Cindy slept, too. I stayed awake and alert at stops, checking the attitudes of the other passengers toward us. All went well.

In my opinion, it doesn't matter which part of Israel travelers visit first. Everything is worth seeing. Make the best plans for the season you're there. There is no single pattern to follow. Tailor-make trips for the benefit and enjoyment of the individuals or team involved. Each of Israel's compass points, North, South, East, and West, as well as its major cities, Tel Aviv, Jerusalem, Haifa, and more, guarantee that time spent provides interesting and memorable experiences.

Here's my fun Dead Sea experience in the summer of 1994. I had come to Israel alone that time and again stayed with Moshe and Tina. (This time she voluntarily silenced her lovely but loud Dutch grandfather clock, so it didn't bong all night above my head.) Tina's high school-age niece and her girlfriend from The Netherlands were also visiting. We discussed options and I agreed to take the girls to Ein Gedi and the Dead Sea because Moshe and Tina had visited both places many times. They would enjoy a day at home.

My younger son Aaron, in medical school in Portland, Oregon, had received a small inheritance from my grandfather. He considered using his funds to join me in Israel to keep me safe, (his idea, not mine), but I had not heard his final decision about coming. I had not seen him for six months and for some reason couldn't reach him by phone in his dorm before I left. Moshe said that if Aaron did arrive mid-morning, he might bring him to us. The girls and I left at 7:30 a.m. but traffic slowed our local bus. We were half-way downtown to Jerusalem's Central Bus Station when Moshe hopped on our bus grinning broadly. We had forgotten our lunches, but he took the bus leaving five minutes after ours and caught up with us, bringing our lunches to our surprise and his delight.

At the Central Station we found the bus to the Dead Sea. We stared through the windows to not miss a thing, seeing scattered Bedouin tents, an oasis, the Dead Sea, and then Qumran where the famous Scrolls were found—all incredible! Then, the bus driver stopped in what seemed the middle of nowhere and dropped us off. A grove of date palms spread below stark mountains. We followed the dusty road into Ein Gedi Nature Park, paid the entrance fee, and began our steep hike upwards. We planned to do the strenuous part of our day early and then cross the highway to the Dead Sea to cool off and relax.

We followed the wide rocky trail toward the green zigzag line slashing the mountainside marking where plants had found water. As we climbed, the narrow stream widened. We reached a first small trickling waterfall where enthusiastic tourists descending from higher up told us that wonderful scenes ahead were worth it! We also enjoyed seeing occasional coneys or hyraxes and agile wild goats or Ibex along the way. As we made our way upward, rushing water sounds grew louder, and suddenly, there we were! Two high gorgeous waterfalls shot out of sheer rock and cascaded down limestone cliffs as people splashed and played in the large pool below.

That's when I learned how the gushing waters form to reach this amazing spot above the Dead Sea. The rugged limestone mountains between here and Bethlehem trap every drop of dew, every rare splash of rain, and filter it through porous rock until it collects in hollow reservoirs below the surface. Staying below ground so it yields no drops to intense surface evaporation, lifegiving waters pool until suddenly the double Ein Gedi waterfalls shoot out from the cliff.

"Ein Gedi" means "fountain of kids or young goats." We saw those healthy Nubian mountain goats everywhere as well as coneys or hyraxes hiding in the rocks. The latter resemble North American marmots but are actually closely related to elephants and manatees!

Israel's future King David must have loved seeing all of these animals scamper over the ridges, and his own heart leaped as he wrote in Psalm 18, He "maketh my feet like hinds' feet, and setteth me upon my high places."

The girls and I enjoyed ourselves until more tourists arrived. After watching the antics of some, and then the more modest behavior of Orthodox Jewish schoolboys and girls, we retraced our steps and crossed the highway to the Dead Sea. The beach site offered freshwater showers to rinse off the salt that encrusts everyone entering the water. We spread out towels. I carefully laid my eyeglasses on mine, and we clambered over burning rocks to enter the water.

It was true! We floated buoyantly in this mineral rich sea. Signs warned against getting water in our eyes, and I soon learned why. I tried to protect my eyes, but one generous-sized German lady splashed a wave my way that I couldn't avoid, and I felt terrible stinging pain! In fact, I'd heard that Dead Sea water in the eyes can cause blindness. My eyes involuntarily snapped shut except for the tears squeezing out. I could barely open them enough to make my way to shore. As I did, I saw the German lady step on my towel and eyeglasses and keep going, bending but not breaking my frames. I crept crablike over large hot uneven rocks to finally reach a freshwater shower. What relief to flood away the clinging salt.

As I stood under the shower, flooding my eyes to save my sight, I saw a regular "Joe Tourist" guy heading my way wearing a blue peaked baseball hat, mirror sunglasses, several days growth of beard, a back pack, "T" shirt, blue knee-length shorts, and Tiva sandals, while carrying a yellow Fodor's *LET'S GO!* travel guide. He came closer and in a heavy Middle Eastern accent said, "I have a question for you! Ver is Tel Aviv?"

I stared. If he was on Israel's side of the Dead Sea, looking for Tel Aviv, he was seriously confused or even a camouflaged terrorist entering from Jordan. I stared harder as this young man grinned and asked, "You're kidding, right?"

His smiled broadened, and I recognized his strong white teeth.

This was my younger son whom I had not seen in six months. "Aaron?"

He laughed and I shrieked, "Aaron Topliff!" as the man pretending to be "Joe Tourist" guffawed and gathered me in his arms for a drenched hug.

My son had totally tricked me and never lets me forget it. During the six months since I'd seen him, my string-bean son had gained ten pounds. Nor had I ever seen him with three days' beard or dressed like a tourist. He laughed so hard and long, he nearly collapsed on the beach.

During his pre-9/11 five-hour layover between planes at London's Heathrow Airport, he had managed to hop on an underground train to visit Buckingham Palace and the Imperial War Museum, meet great people, and race back to Heathrow in time to board his flight to Israel. He had flown British Air and reached Tel Aviv at 6 a.m. Too excited to sleep, he bused to Jerusalem and negotiated the local transit system well enough to reach Moshe and Tina's home without phoning for directions. He knocked on their door, incredibly pleased with himself.

Moshe told Aaron that the girls and I had just left and that since Aaron had proved himself to be a skilled traveler, he could catch a later bus and surprise us at a Dead Sea resort. Moshe correctly guessed we'd be at the first one opposite Ein Gedi. He packed my son a lunch and sent him off.

Aaron was ecstatic to surprise me. I was literally the first person he saw at the first beach he tried! After my welcoming shrieks and hugs, he entered the mineral-rich water and floated for an hour with his hat on for sun protection, still frequently cackling with laughter.

My son connected to Israel's scenery and atmosphere with the fierce love of any native-born Sabra. Plus, his given name fit right in. I loved showing him around the land of milk and honey.

The main agricultural crops Israeli settlers initially concentrated on were olives, grapes, and citrus. World-famous Jaffa oranges thrive. Dates are in high production. Today, the nation is a worldclass exporter of fresh cut flowers flown to global centers, only placing behind Ecuador, Malaysia, Italy, Kenya, Belgium, Ethiopia, and India in production. In 2020, The Flower Council, an Israeli company formed by farmers to handle exports, is the biggest, most successful exporter of flowers grown by residents in the West Bank and the Gaza Strip.

## Israel's National Parks, Historic Sites, and Nature Reserves

Israel has wisely created many National Parks, historic sites, and nature reserves. The six most visited are Caesarea, Ein Gedi/ En Gedi, Masada, Mount Carmel, Beth Shan/Beit Shean, (one of the world's largest archaeological sites), and Gan HaShlosha/the Sachne in northern Galilee with warm springs for swimming.

Shaded by lush palms and green lawns, its pools stay at a temperature of 82F/28C year-round. Find information on any National Parks, Historic Sites and Nature Reserves online.

Each park is maintained and operated by Israel's National Nature and Parks Authority. Instead of paying high entrance fees to visit them individually, a helpful sales clerk at Korazim/Chorazin urged us to save by buying an annual Parks Pass that allows lower entrance prices. Visit any three parks, or multiples of three, and save on your costs. In fact, the brochure invites, "Buy an Israel Nature and Parks Authority subscription for unlimited free entry to 55 National Parks and Reserves." Find full details at https://en.parks.org.il/

National parks, such as Tel Megiddo, Ashkelon, Beit She'an, and Kursi are also archaeological sites. The Alexander Stream, Mount Carmel, and Hurshat Tal National Parks focus on preserving local flora and fauna. Several parks and nature reserves offer camping. The most popular National Parks are Yarkon, Caesarea, Ein Gedi/En Gedi, and Tel Dan. I've been to all but Yarkon. Travelers will not go wrong by visiting all and then choosing a favorite.

Israel's four hundred nature reserves protect over twenty-five hundred species of indigenous wild plants, thirty-two fish species, one hundred mammal species, and over five hundred and thirty bird species.

## Religious Sites

No one forgets their first time arriving in and seeing any country's special sights. I've had conversations with others who've visited Israel, and we find our first impressions and experiences more unique and outstanding there than in most nations. That was especially true for Cindy and me as we first encountered the scenes of Jesus' life and ministry.

Again, Tina had contacts with Christian friends in the Galilee area from Finland, Germany, and France who lived quietly in Tiberias in a large and lovely former Arab bakery offering guest rooms in a building in their extensive garden. They did not advertise. Guests came by referral. It was worth the trip to meet these fine people and share life histories and sing songs together. In fact, we've stayed in touch since. Cindy and I were only there a few days on that first trip and did our best to see the major sites.

An idealist, I was then an unpaid volunteer Bible college teacher. That produced little predictable income but taught me shoestring economics. Cindy worked in an accounting firm in the nearest town, so had regular income. It complicated things that we'd reached Tiberias on a Thursday evening before Friday Sabbath/Shabbat. To stretch funds and enjoy the scenery, we bought one-way tickets the next morning to cross the Sea of Galilee on a small tour boat. Jewish buses don't run on the Sabbath. We planned to walk along the other side of the lake until sunset when life resumed and Jewish buses would run again.

The boat's other passengers were a Dutch-Reformed church group from California. Their Arab Christian guide became alarmed when Cindy and I gave him our one-way tickets.

"How will you return?" he asked, frowning. "What is your plan?"

"We'll be fine," I insisted. "We'll walk and explore the other side until sunset and then catch a Jewish bus."

He didn't like that idea and shook his head. "We're six hundred feet below sea level here. You'll get sunstroke." He approached the tour group's pastor.

That pastor came to us. "Here's our itinerary. We'll drive completely around the lake and see all the major sites, then drive to Lebanon's border and past the Golan Heights. We'll return to Tiberias by dark and drop you off wherever you need to go." He studied our faces. "How would you like to join us?"

I knew that the minimum cost for such tours was then $50 U.S. each. Cindy had the funds; I didn't.

"That sounds wonderful, but what would you need to charge us?" I asked.

His blue eyes twinkled. "Do you think you could each give one smile?"

Could we? Cindy and I beamed sunshine that whole day long. On board the luxury bus, our new church tour friends shared fresh fruit, granola bars, and cold bottles of water as we exchanged addresses and invited them to visit Canada. We visited Capernaum where Jesus taught in the synagogue and prayed away Peter's mother-in-law's high fever so she immediately rose up and, like any good Jewish mother, served dinner.

We stopped at Tabgha, the traditional location for another significant event in the life of Jesus. Located on the Sea of Galilee's northwestern shore, on the slopes of the Mount of Beatitudes, this area was earlier called "Heptapegon," a Greek word translated as "seven springs." Tabgha is the Arab translation.

From there we climbed the Mount of Beatitudes where over five thousand men, women, and children had gathered to hear Jesus teach, staying and listening for three days because they were hungry for more than food. At the end of that time, Jesus used little to make much, miraculously multiplying five loaves and two fishes to feed them all. Some translations say they didn't nibble but ate all they wanted and the disciples still gathered twelve baskets full. Along with the California pastor and his group, we sat on that same hillside overlooking the same sea.

By contacting the site in advance, the pastor had planned ahead and reserved a private area for us to share time together. He distributed Bibles and assigned verses for us to read aloud from Matthew 5 describing that event. My verse was Chapter 5:6, "Blessed are those who hunger and thirst for righteousness, for they shall be filled and abundantly satisfied."

In that moment, I felt that the living Jesus Himself stood with us. His arm swept around the breathtaking countryside inviting us to take in the view as He said, "Welcome to my land. This is My home. Enjoy. Let me show you around."

He seemed joyful and personable, His voice warm. My throat thickened. In the middle of reading my verse, I uncharacteristically burst into tears, overwhelmed by such unexpected caring love in this place so central to the ministry of Jesus—aware of Him fulfilling the name Emmanuel, God with us, in every sense. He was the powerful historic Jesus yet fully present with us on that day to meet our needs.

That boat and bus ride was a divine appointment. I make a point of keeping trip diaries and travel notes to share with others who cannot come on trips with me. The details and emotions of such experiences are not forgotten.

**The Jesus Trail** is a 40-mile (65-km.) path beginning in Nazareth retracing the footsteps of Jesus past many key places of His ministry. Highlights include Cana, Migdal, Tabgha, St. Peter's Primacy, and the Mount of Beatitudes before reaching Capernaum, the center where Jesus based his Galilean ministry. In March 2000, Pope John Paul II came to celebrate a youth mass on a hillside near Capernaum above the Sea of Galilee where 50,000 pilgrims from around the world gathered to celebrate mass during his jubilee millennium pilgrimage to Israel.

**The Dome of the Rock**, the third holiest site to Muslims, is on the site where Israel's First and Second Temples were built and destroyed and where the Jews plan to build the Third Temple. The Temple Mount is also the most Holy Site for Jews and Christians. Christians believe this is where Jesus will return via the Eastern (Golden) Gate presently blocked shut by Muslims centuries ago to keep that from happening.

**The Church of the Holy Sepulcher** is considered Christianity's oldest site by those accepting it as the place of Christ's crucifixion, burial, and resurrection. Built by Emperor Constantine from 325-326 AD/CE, it is administered today by six Christian churches (not always peacefully).

In 2022, for the first time, systematic excavation of the church courtyard and other areas is being led by Giorgio Piras of the

Sapienza University. "We don't know what is beneath the floor... so we don't know what we shall find. But it should be at least some remains of Constantine's church." The repairs and excavations come after nearly 30 years of discussion between the three main Christian denominations—Greek Orthodox, Catholics, and Armenians—that share custodial authority for the church.

**The Church of Saint Peter Gallicantu** is on the eastern slope of Mt. Zion just beyond the Old City walls. It is where Jesus, after being scourged and condemned to death, is said to have been held in prison all night in a stone cell deep under Caiaphas, the Jewish High Priest's, home. It is also believed to be the location where Peter denied the Lord and is how the church was named. Gallicantu means where the rooster crowed.

**The Via Dolorosa**—Through the years, location of the actual route of the Via Dolorosa has shifted very slightly as control of the Old City's Christian holy sites has changed hands. Beginning at the Antonia Fortress, the path leads around 2,000 feet to the Church of the Holy Sepulcher. The current route includes fourteen stations, marking special locations along the journey. Nine stations are found along the way to the Sepulcher. The remaining five are inside the Holy Sepulcher itself.

**The Garden Tomb**, uncovered in 1867, has been researched by such eminent archaeologists as Gabriel Barkay, finder of the pre-Solomon era silver priestly benediction scroll. The garden's location just beyond Jerusalem's Old City walls is the other site where many believe the crucifixion, burial, and resurrection of Jesus took place. Many details closely match the Biblical record.

Travelers are encouraged to explore and enjoy both The Garden Tomb and the Church of the Holy Sepulcher to reach their own conclusions.

Bob Allen's color slides and brochures had prepared me for the Garden Tomb ahead of time. I knew it was near the Damascus Gate off Nablus Road beyond Old Jerusalem's walls. He had told me the best view of Golgotha's hill, "The Place of the Skull," was from the nearby Arab bus station. The tomb is hard to find unless you know where to look. One small sign marks its location near heavy wooden gates that remain closed during off hours. Its website says to book a visit, especially if you want to reserve a small sitting area for reflection, but I've found that is not necessary. Just talk to the staff at the entrance window when entering and they will arrange what you need. Their hours of operation are posted online. By necessity, they were often closed during the Covid and variant pandemics, but thankfully that is over now. They are not open on Sundays.

The narrow rock-walled approach is Conrad Schick Street named for a mid-nineteenth century German archaeologist and Protestant missionary. The four-hundred foot lane off of Nablus Rd. is not wide enough to turn cars around in as I learned on a later visit. Thankfully, we had the help of Sammy, the cheerful Arab Christian olive wood vendor outside the entrance gate who expertly backed up our car up for us. We joked that the rock walls were so near, they brushed off our car's dust and it no longer needed a wash.

But that first time, the moment I entered the Garden Tomb, the sounds of the city fell away. Nothing prepared me for the beauty and atmosphere inside. Exquisite gardens and flowering trees lined walkways. Pilgrims from many lands sang praises in dozens of languages, but as I neared the empty tomb with the heavy stone rolled away, a holy hush fell. I bent and entered, seeing where the stone niche had been carved deeper for a man of taller than average height. He was crucified and laid there until sin's penalty was met and heaven acknowledged full payment by raising him again. My tears flowed as the reality of His resurrection and an empty tomb stole my breath. When I calmed, I joined those singing along the paths and drank in the beauty and victory proclaimed through the vivid colors and sweetness of so many blooming flowers and trees. That experience imprinted my thirsty heart forever.

**The Old Jericho Road.** I wish I could give an exact location for a place I would love travelers to see on the Old Jericho Road, Highway 1, descending from Jerusalem to Jericho. Biblical Resources took us to a spot midway on the northern side of that highway to show us sheep and goat trails where shepherds have led their flocks and herds from early times. We stopped at what appeared to be an active corral with a foundation base of stones with interwoven branches above for walls, and finally briars and thorns high up to prevent foxes and other predators from entering. The Psalms tell us that David the shepherd boy killed a lion and bear while protecting his sheep. In his day, lions did live in the Pride of Jordan area where the Sea of Galilee empties into the Jordan River.

Our guide drew attention to the fact that the stone corral had no door or gate.

"What do you think they used?" He asked. We looked at each other. We had no idea.

"The shepherd folded his own body into the opening," our guide said. "He was the living door the Apostle John describes in his Gospel, chapter 10. He stayed there all night so no enemy could get past."

His words gave us chills. I wish every visitor could see that place.

Historic Sites Archaeology

Endless research and study sites are found all throughout Israel displaying the physical record of the peoples who have invaded, occupied, or passed through this amazing hub of three continents. The list of occupiers and/or conquerors includes Nabatean Arabs, Canaanites, Israelites, Phoenicians, Persians, Hasmoneans, Romans, Byzantines, Arabs, Crusaders, Ottomans, and the British.

For example, remains of the Nabatean Arab civilization display irrigation marvels that enabled them to grow vineyards in the Negev Desert in ways that amaze and inspire us today. They carved Petra out of solid sandstone cliffs. Using the Old Testament as his guide, American Rabbi and archaeologist, Nelson Glueck, rediscovered King Solomon's copper mines, over 1500 additional ancient sites, and wrote fascinating books about the area and people that are still excellent reading today.

**Gezer, Hazor, and Megiddo** are the tel mounds of three ancient chariot cities worth visiting. Gezer, where a school boy's surviving clay calendar of the year's farming events is on display, Hazor, a Canaanite stronghold put to the sword and burned by Joshua as one of his major victories in conquering the Promised Land, and Megiddo, (Armageddon in Greek), a vital fortress intersecting two major trade and military routes, all share the unique city gate design attributed to King Solomon. These gates have three-rooms on each side of the entrance for a total of six-chambers forty-eight feet wide. The three sites have identical water cistern systems measuring seven-meters deep with staircases inside city walls and fortyfive-degree tunnels that angle down to their water supply if the city is put under siege.

**Tel Megiddo** is an especially well-developed national site for people to enjoy windows into history through well-excavated ruins, fascinating models, and excellent audio and visual talks. Many tour groups pass through the site daily with their guides giving detailed lectures to their groups. Most don't mind interested individuals stepping closer to listen. Overhearing one outstanding guide at Megiddo years ago is how I first heard and met Arie Bar David, the gentleman I consider Israel's best and most interesting guide. After initially hearing him at Megiddo on my first trip, I continued seeing him at other sites and church meetings, so have kept my eyes and ears open ever since by reading more of his blogs and appreciating his online videos and teachings. You can find many references to him and interviews online.

**Acre/Akko** is a UNESCO World Heritage Site showcasing Israel's varied history during rule by the Romans, Ottomans, Crusaders, Mamelukes, Byzantines, and British. Like Haifa, this city also demonstrates the successful coexistence of Jewish, Christian, and Muslim populations together.

**Beth Shan/Beit She'an** on Mount Gilboa in the northern Jordan River Valley is a vast archaeological site with ruins dating to Roman and Byzantine times but also reflecting earlier Egyptian control. After defeat by the Philistines, the bodies of King Saul and his three sons were hung on the city's walls until they were rescued for proper burial by the men of Jabesh-Gilead and lamented by David in II Samuel, chapter 1.

**Maritima Palestina/Caesarea Palestina** is the ancient Roman city and harbor built by Herod the Great on the Mediterranean in the first century BC/BCE. Its breakwaters are built from lime mixed with volcanic ash to form amazing underwater concrete first invented by the Romans. An aqueduct carried water nearly ten miles (16-km.) from springs in the northeastern hills. The Apostle Paul was imprisoned there for two years, charged with being a follower of Jesus, until his appeal to Caesar took him to Rome where the Lord had told him he would give testimony as he had in Jerusalem (Acts 23).

**Hezekiah's Water Tunnel** (or the Siloam Tunnel) in Jerusalem's City of David National Park was built by Judah's King Hezekiah in 701 BC/BCE to guarantee a water supply when the Assyrian Army advanced and threatened siege. The amazingly engineered 1750-foot tunnel connected the Gihon Spring to the Pool of Siloam inside the Old City walls. The tunnel is one of the City of David's most famous features. Those entering will see the marks on the wall where the two work teams met within inches of each other after digging the considerable distance from either end through solid rock.

**Masada** is the massive Dead Sea mountain fortress build by King Herod where Jewish zealots resisted long siege by Roman forces and preferred mass suicide in 66 AD/CE rather than be captured and enslaved by the Romans.

**Megiddo** (Armageddon in Greek meaning "Hill of Megiddo") is an ancient hill fortress overlooking the Valley of Jezreel/Plain of Esdraelon which controls the trading routes connecting Egypt with Mesopotamia and the northwest-southeast road joining early Phoenician cities with Jerusalem and the Jordan River Valley. Today, Tel Megiddo is an outstanding national park and UNESCO world heritage site. As described in the Archaeology section, its fortifications and signature city gate are attributed to King Solomon. The site was further expanded under King Ahab's rule.

**Pella** located in the Perean foothills of the Jordan River in northwestern Jordan. Jesus, while looking over the temple mount shortly before his death, prophesied that its stones would be thrown down within a generation. He warned that residents should flee Jerusalem to the mountains when they saw the Roman armies surrounding the city. This admonition of Jesus is found in each of the Synoptic Gospels (Matthew 24; Mark 13, and Luke 21). Perhaps Jesus visited Pella during his visit to the Decapolis (Mark 7:31) and Perea (Matthew 19:1; Mark 10:1), and recalling its secure location, cryptically referred to it in this prophecy. Eusebius's *Church History* (3.5.3) recounts that the Jewish followers of Jesus heeded his warning and fled to Pella for safety before Jerusalem's destruction.

Today, Pella sits outside Tabaqat Fahl, twenty miles south of the Sea of Galilee. The University of Sydney has been conducting excavations at Pella since 1979. Remains from the Natufian through the Islamic period have been discovered –a period spanning over 10,000 years. But my interest was on structures that would have existed in the late first century AD/CE. There are remnants of a Roman odeon, bathhouse, and necropolis. Roman milestones found in the nearby hills show that roads directly connected Pella with the important Decapolis city of Gerasa, modern Jerash.

**Shiloh/Shilo**—from the time Israel conquered the land and Joshua divided it among the twelve tribes, the Tabernacle resided in Shiloh until the death of Eli the High Priest. Three times a year the faithful traveled there bringing offerings. Today Tel Shilo is a popular tourist and archaeological site where the spiritual life of the Jewish people was centered for 369 years in the 11th and 12th centuries BC/BCE.

**The Via Dolorosa**—Through the years, the actual route of the Via Dolorosa has shifted slightly as control of the Old City's Christian holy sites has changed hands. Beginning at the Antonia Fortress, the path leads nearly 2,000 feet to the Church of the Holy Sepulcher. The current route includes fourteen stations, marking special locations along the journey. Nine stations are found along the way to the Sepulcher. The remaining five are inside the Church of the Holy Sepulcher itself.

**The Western Wall** on Jerusalem's Temple Mount is considered Judaism's holiest site. It is a surviving part of Herod's Second Temple destroyed by Roman General Titus in 70 AD/CE before he became Emperor. Some derisively call it "The Wailing Wall" because Jewish people sometimes weep there while praying for Messiah to come. However, the correct name found on direction signs throughout the Old City is "The Western Wall."

Although it was not accessible on my early trips, visitors may now easily enter and tour The Western Wall (Kotel) Tunnels to see their impressive, extensive construction. Part of the wall's underground portion is believed to be nearest the Second Temple's Holy of Holies. A number of faithful Jewish women and men are usually found as close as possible to that spot praying for Messiah to come and for the eventual building of the Third Temple. Now, people may also view the Western Wall online and take tours remotely by live-streaming from anywhere. Check the Western Wall Heritage Foundation's online site to locate tours, times, and to buy tickets.

When it's not possible to visit Israel due to personal situations or things like Covid and its variant strains, more livestream and Zoom tours of destinations are becoming available. One offered free by Jerusalem Tours International is at this current link

https://www.israel365.com/virtual-pilgrimage-to-israel/

I had seen dramatic photos of the Western Wall that stirred my heart before being visiting there in person, but nothing prepared me for standing near this part of the Second Temple built by King Herod in 19 BC/BCE where Jesus walked and prayed before my arrival. Its massive limestone blocks turn gold in the setting sun. In Matthew 24, Jesus told his disciples that the time would come when, "There shall not be left here one stone upon another." The largest foundation block is 42 feet (12.8 meters) long, 11 feet (3.4 meters) high, and over fourteen feet (4.3 meters) deep with an estimated weight of 660 tons.

Men pray at the wall on their side of the divided area and women on their side in what scripture calls the "Court of the Women." Both sexes usually keep their heads covered in respect. Since the early eighteenth century, petitioners have written brief prayers on small papers to wedge into cracks between the stones as the Divine Presence is believed to dwell there. As papers fall, they are bagged, saved, and moved to the underground wall tunnel location nearest to the Holy of Holies where faithful Jewish people pray.

Each time I go, I add prayers for loved ones and world situations. Last time, I was busy helping my team and didn't get my list written. But as I stood there, head covered, I heard myself pray, "Lord, I believe, help my unbelief. Lord, I pray, teach me to pray. Lord, I praise; teach me to praise. Lord, I love; teach me to love ..." Those words stay with me.

On Palm Sunday, when Jesus rode into Jerusalem on the colt of a donkey, people shouted, "Hosanna!" (Blessed is he who comes in the name of the Lord.) When Pharisees told Jesus to rebuke his disciples, He answered, "I tell you, if these were silent, the very stones would cry out" (Luke 19:39-40). Throughout Israel, and especially in Jerusalem, the ancient stones still bring their message to life again.

**Rabin Square** (formerly Israel Kings in Tel Aviv' Square) was renamed after the assassination of Israel's Prime Minister Yitzhak Rabin in 1995.

**Yad Vashem**, near Mount Herzl, is the world's most complete Holocaust Museum. Admission is free although donations are appreciated. Paid parking and a cafeteria are available—plan a minimum stay of three to four hours to see it all and the displays are so impacting, allow yourself time afterward to recover.

**Castel National Park**—a simple hike uphill from Yad Vashem brings visitors to Castel National Park to learn of the fascinating events that happened there in Operation Nachshon's key battles during the 1948 Arab-Israeli War.

**Jerusalem** is an ancient city now surrounded by a modern one with nearly a million residents. During its five-thousand-year history, Jerusalem has known long periods of conflict under the rule of Jews, Greeks, Romans, Byzantines, Muslims, Christians, Ottomans, and the British. Jerusalem lies at the heart of three world religions and is holy to Jews, Christians, and Muslims. While its religious history gives the city great importance, the Israeli-Arab conflict also makes it some of the world's most contested real estate.

**Judea and Samaria**, Israel's heartland, are known to Arabs as the West Bank (of the Jordan River). Israel is the governing force, but the territories are ruled and represented by the Palestinian Authority. There is not yet a unified political leadership over the Arabs living in the West Bank and Gaza.

Major West Bank Sites

**Beersheba** contains ancient Tel Beersheba and Abraham's well, sacred to all three faiths. Lakiya, a nearby modern Bedouin village, offers "Embroideries of the Desert" for sale including many items and even beautiful hand-made rugs handwoven by Bedouins using their feet with shells in their toes. We were pleased to shop there on our 2023 trip.

**Hebron** houses the tomb of Abraham sacred to three religions. It is the second-most important spiritual location in Israel after Jerusalem.

**Jericho** is a large Arab city in the West Bank east of Jerusalem and west of the Jordan River. It is believed to be one of the world's oldest continuously occupied cities with a protective wall 5 to 6.6 feet thick, 12 to 17 feet high, and with a 28-foot tall tower. The city was annexed and ruled by Jordan from 1949 to 1967 but returned to Israel in 1967.

**Nablus**, the largest commercial and cultural center in the West Bank with UN-run schools was formerly biblical Shechem or Sichem.

**Ramallah** was historically an Arab-Christian town but is now where the Palestinian Authority is based.

A British lady also staying with Moshe and Tina recommended we visit Baal Hazor. It's mentioned several times in scripture and is where Joshua led the Israelites to defeat combined Canaanite troops. He later looted and burned the city as archaeological evidence shows. It is one of the three Solomonic treasure cities described in this book's Megiddo section, also sharing the distinctive triple gate and deep-water cistern.

We loved our time there. At the end of a hot humid afternoon at a site far below sea level, when it was time to return to Moshe and Tinas' home, we stood at a public bus stop along with two young IDF soldiers. They seemed shy but said they were single. They asked if I was Cindy's mother and if she was single. Hearing she was available, one used a pick-up line I'd never heard before.

"You have beautiful fingernails. May I see them?"

She extended one hand and the next thing we knew, he held her hand at length, gazing into her eyes.

"Meet me Tuesday in Beersheba at the camel market," he said.

"The camel market?" I asked.

"Yes, that's where camels are used to pay dowries for beautiful brides and marriages are arranged."

We laughed while Cindy gently extracted her hand. "What's the going bride rate?" I asked.

"At least twenty-five healthy camels. But for someone as beautiful as her, considerably higher."

Just then, our bus arrived in a cloud of dust, and we were saved further negotiations. Later, I asked other Israelis about bride prices at the camel market. I learned the most desirable brides are plump blondes. The going rate was then thirty camels! We later visited Beersheba, but not on camel market day, so we don't know what price Cindy might have fetched. Now happily married, her North American husband says he would have beat the highest offer.

A few days later, we attended a conference in a Jerusalem hotel and walked through the dining room. A handsome young Arab waiter was setting tables for a banquet. He took one look at Cindy, snatched a packet of sugar, and thrust it into her hand.

"This is for you. You are lovely, sweeter than sugar. Meet me here at 9 p.m. when I get off work or I will *kill* myself."

This was said with great feeling and deeply expressive brown eyes.

We did not return at 9 p.m. and didn't read his obituary, so we trust the waiter survived. Cindy had that effect on people.

I learned later that one of my college students had spent six months volunteering on a Kibbutz in Israel. Things are hopefully different now, but as an outgoing American Mid-westerner, my student was used to friendly conversations while looking other speakers in the eyes. That didn't work well on one occasion. A young man she worked with and his friend came to her to formalize their engagement.

"Our engagement?" She sputtered. "What do you mean?"

"In our culture, when you look someone fully in the eyes, you are accepting their words. He asked you to marry him."

Kibbutz leaders helped explain my student's way out of the situation, but she conversed less openly after that and walked with downcast eyes.

Varied Spellings

Travelers are wise to be approximate and flexible in reading maps and location signs in Israel. Spellings may vary widely from how they are recorded in Bible History and compared to how they appear now. Sound them out and you may recognize something familiar. Our minds crave exactness, but it was fun to discover that the road we took from Nazareth to Tiberias passed through Kana, the same Cana where Jesus performed his first miracle of turning water into wine. Or that Sedom, (also Sdom and Sodom), besides being the city both the Bible and Quran say God destroyed with burning sulfur because of its sins, is the site of a potash mine today at the Dead Sea's southern end and where Israelis believe they have discovered the world's longest salt cave.

I describe the process for recognizing ancient place names among modern spellings as letting your eyes go slightly out of focus to see what other name possibilities exist. Besides Sedom/Sdom/Sodom, other location spelling variations include Be'er Sheva/Lakiya , Beersheba/Laqye, Jaffa/Joppa/Yafo, Ein Dor/Endor, and many more. Recognizing them is like following a treasure map and finding gold.

Historic dates also are written differently in Israel than in most of the rest of the world. Instead of "before Christ" being abbreviated as BC, it is written as "BCE, Before the Common Era," (or as some say, "Before the Common Error") Instead of Anno Domini, "in the year of our Lord (the year Jesus was born) being abbreviated AD, in Israel it is written as CE (Common Era), although some insist that CE stands for "Common Error."

On my first trip to Israel, I spent thirty-six days traveling throughout the entire country. I'd had a full year to study and prepare before going, but there were still many more things it would have been good to know and understand ahead of time. For example, in its early years, Israel was almost entirely a nation of immigrants making Aliyah, "to go up or return" to the Jewish homeland as the Bible instructs. People native born in the land are called Sabras after the local cactus we call prickly pear with its thorny thick outer skin covering but sweet, soft heart. Immigration and Aliyah continue, but the statistical proportions are changing. As of July 2020, 70.3% of Israel's Jewish population is native-born, and often second or third-generation.

## Branches of Judaism, Government, Cultural Explanations

In university, I enjoyed friendships with people from several branches of Judaism but wasn't clear on the distinctions. I know now that identity clues are visible through variations in dress, hats, language, etc., to help us know people's beliefs, associations, and much more.

**Orthodox Judaism** is defined by the belief that the Torah (Teaching or Law) that Adonai or Jehovah gave Moses on Mount Sinai was transmitted faithfully in the Pentateuch (the first five written books of the Bible) as well as in the Oral tradition. Its changeless instructions and requirements are to be literally carried out.

**Ultra-Orthodox** is the term applied to religious Jews who wear traditional (unusual to us) outfits that set them apart visually from the non-religious world.

**Reform Judaism** (also known as Liberal or Progressive Judaism) is a modern denomination believing that faith evolves instead of being unchanging. It values ethical aspects over ceremonial ones and puts less emphasis on ritual and personal observance than does Orthodox Judaism. It views faith as a continuing revelation influenced by human reason and intellect instead of being based solely on God's revelation on Mount Sinai. Its policy is inclusiveness and acceptance rather than inflexible law. It embraces progressive political and social agendas. Today the movement's largest center is in North America.

**Jewish Secularism** is a variation on the theme reflecting the non-religious Jewish people and their work. They may celebrate traditional Jewish holidays as historic and nature festivals. Lifecycle events, like births, marriages, and deaths may be marked in secular ways.

**Humanistic Judaism** celebrates the human aspects of Jewish culture without its supernatural foundation. It embraces a human-centered philosophy combining rational thinking with a deep connection to the Jewish people and culture but doesn't fully accept the other practices of Judaism.

Many Jews in Israel practice a popular style of Orthodox Judaism called "Modern Orthodoxy." This gives more credibility to biblical interpretation of the law than the Talmudic writings (the oral interpretation) of the law.

**Conservative Judaism** is considered midway between Orthodox and Reformed Judaism and accepts traditional practices. Some Conservative Jews keep Kosher and uphold tenets of the Mosaic Law—but not as strictly as the Orthodox. Conservative Judaism is mainly practiced among Jews living outside of Israel. Masorti is traditional Judaism that like Conservative Judaism is mainly practiced in Israel.

In synagogues, Orthodox Jews have separate areas in services for men and women. This is true at Orthodox weddings and observances as well.

Jewish people refer to non-Jews as Gentiles. Some use the derogatory word "Goyim" instead. On my first trip to Israel, I didn't realize how unacceptable it was for pious Jews to interact with non Jews, let alone with non-Jewish women, until I boarded a bus one morning to ride from Gilo to Jerusalem's Central Bus Station.

The green Egged Company city bus was almost full. I spotted one narrow space in the last row across the very back of the bus. Four men already sat there but it looked like one more could squeeze in. The only other empty spot was in the seat immediately behind the driver where an Orthodox rabbi occupied the half by the window, leaving one vacant seat for me. I guessed him to be in his mid-sixties dressed in full black garb, hat, curly ear locks, long black coat, and dark shoes and stockings. I quickly sat, grateful for a seat rather than standing in the aisle grasping the overhead rail as the lurching bus navigated curved streets and hills toward downtown.

However, commotion began the instant I sat. Although the bus was weaving, the rabbi stood in a rush. His hands grabbed both edges of his black coat and flapped them briskly at me, as if shaking off dust. Without speaking, he whirled past me and down the bus's aisle to the last row where he squeezed in among the four men there. No one else boarded before we reached downtown. I enjoyed my seat and scooted to the window to enjoy the view. I realized I had experienced a modern-day version of Jesus's words in Matthew 10 that if a town or house was found to be unworthy, his followers should depart and "shake off the dust" of their feet. The rabbi's rejection did not wound me. I enjoyed my ride and appreciated the unobstructed view.

The only other time I've experienced something like that has been on international flights between Israel and North America. Apparently, Orthodox Jewish rabbis must read, pray, and recite certain scripture portions at set times, even on long flights. I've seen them stand in plane aisles to complete the specific requirements but usually without inconveniencing others. However, on a recent trip when friends and I flew from Charles de Gaulle Airport, Paris, to Tel Aviv, a rabbi observing his ritual added to a serious problem.

It was the day before Rosh Hashanah, the Jewish New Year, and the beginning of Judaism's High Holy Days leading to Yom Kippur. Our plane was filled with eager travelers returning to celebrate with families. Suddenly an older gentleman sitting with his wife three or four rows ahead of us slumped into unconsciousness. We didn't notice immediately because the man's wife and the responding flight attendant stayed calm. Passengers continued chatting, and we still didn't notice until the attendant used the overhead to request help from someone with medical expertise. The three young medical students sitting behind me caught on.

"It's probably his heart," one said, pointing forward. "Or a stroke," another answered.

Because my two sons are doctors, I paid attention. Our plane quieted except for the rabbi standing three-fourths of the way back in the aisle who continued his observance. Two first responders muscled a bulky stretcher forward past him with difficulty from somewhere in the back. The rabbi did not relinquish his position. The helpers reached the unmoving passenger, stretched him out, covered him with a blanket, and struggled back down the aisle to place him in a secluded spot where a doctor on board attended him.

Unbelievably, the rabbi still did not move even when attendants quietly spoke to him. He continued reading and reciting as if unaware of the critical events around him. The ill man was slight and weighed little. Thankfully, the stretcher bearers squeezed past.

Because I teach college world geography, I always love studying the landscape below my plane window. I saw the curve of France's southern coastline as we reached the Mediterranean and noticed our plane change direction. I recognized the unmistakable boot shape of southern Italy, which we should not have seen on our more southerly route. Then our plane lost altitude as we descended over the rugged mountains of central Greece although our in-flight magazine map showed we should not have come close to Greece's mainland at all. "We'll make an emergency landing in Athens," I told a friend with me seconds before the loudspeaker announced that same news.

We touched down in Athens and the unmoving man and his wife were whisked away by ambulance. Our pilots filed a new flight plan for approval and we refueled, which all took time. Instead of reaching Tel Aviv at 4:30 p.m., we landed after 9 p.m. We wished and prayed for our fellow passenger's recovery but had no way of knowing his outcome.

Maybe I don't understand the importance and time sensitivity of religious ritual. While I have great respect and thankfulness for Judaism's foundations of my faith, those of us watching the rabbi follow his regimen while a life and death struggle took place around him were appalled.

Key Jewish Definitions

A **Tetragram** (Greek), sometimes called Tetragrammaton, consists of the four Hebrew consonant letters in the biblical name of the God of Israel. Jews are forbidden to speak it. His name is not to be spoken by mortals, which is why the Tetragrammaton is represented by four unspeakable consonants. From left to right, the consonants are *yud hey vav hey*. Jews instead are to say "Adonai," meaning "Lord," or Ha Shem, meaning "the name."

**The Shema**—observant Jews consider the "shema" meaning "to hear" to be at the heart of Judaism. These verses from Deuteronomy 6:4-6 are to be recited three times daily as a religious commandment or mitzvah. 4 "Hear, O Israel: The Lord our God is one Lord: 5And thou shalt love the Lord thy God with all thine heart, and with all thy soul, and with all thy might."

A **synagogue** is a Jewish house of worship with a large space for prayer and usually smaller rooms for study. Some have a separate room for Torah study, called the beth midrash. Wherever they are, synagogues are centers of Jewish life serving as places of prayer, schools, town halls, and community centers.

A **minyan** is a quorum of ten men (or in some Conservative and

Reformed synagogues, men and women) above the age of thirteen required for traditional Jewish public worship. In Orthodox synagogues, the quorum is men only.

Primary Branches of Judaism

**Ashkenazi Jews** are a dispersion (diaspora) of Jews from Israel who gathered in the Rhineland Valley and France before migrating east to Slavic Poland, Lithuania, Russia, etc. after the 11th to 13th century Crusades. Two and a half million Israelis are Ashkenazi Jews from Eastern Europe. Formerly, in addition to Hebrew, most spoke Yiddish and/or Judeo-Spanish. Today, fewer Ashkenazi Jews speak Yiddish. It's considered an old language.

Some ultra-Orthodox Ashkenazi Jews do speak Yiddish within their families.

**Sephardic (or Hispanic) Jews** make up most of the remaining Jewish population. They are descendants of Jews who lived in the Iberian Peninsula and North Africa from near the end of the Roman Empire until their persecution and expulsion at the end of the 15th century AD/CE under Spain's King Ferdinand and Queen Isabella.

**Hasidic (Chassidic) Judaism** is a religious group that arose as a charismatic spiritual revival in Ukraine during the 18th century and spread through Eastern Europe. They are characterized by joyful singing and dancing.

**The Hasidim, followers of Hasidism**, interact in independent sects called "courts" or dynasties headed by hereditary Rebbes (Rabbis). Key traits are reverence and submission, as the rebbe is the spiritual authority with whom followers' bond to grow close to God.

**Bar Mitzvah**, meaning "son of the commandment," is the coming of age initiation ceremony for Jewish boys usually age twelve in Israel but sometimes age thirteen outside of Israel which entitles the young person to the rights and obligations of Jewish adulthood. If from an Orthodox Jewish family, young men will likely begin wearing *tefillin* (phylacteries) on a daily basis afterward, participate in synagogue services, and take their place in the Jewish community.

Celebration, feasting, and lavish gift-giving are part of this major life milestone.

**Bat Mitzvah** is the religious coming of age ceremony for Jewish girls aged twelve in Israel but sometimes thirteen outside of Israel. It means "daughter of the commandment" and also marks the age of girls reaching religious maturity to become accountable for their actions and to take their place in the Jewish community.

Distinctive Clothing

Specific garb worn by Jewish men and women signals many aspects of their religious, social, and/or marital status. Among Ashkenazi and Sephardic branches of Judaism, Tzniut is the term describing the character trait of modesty and the Orthodox Jewish laws defining it.

Modest clothing fashion is the rule for all aspects of dress among religious women. The many steps required to achieve modesty raise it to an art form. Printed and online instructions include lessons like, "How to tie my Sinar Tichel, How to wrap a Head Scarf, Hair Snood, Head Covering, Scarf, Bandana, Apron," etc.

The manner in which each is worn reveals information about the wearer. Google sites like Etsy show items for sale, how to tie them, etc.

Orthodox women cover their hair with hats, scarves, or wigs (*sheitels*). They believe their hair is to be covered and seen only by their husbands in the privacy of their bedrooms. Doing so is a sign of fidelity and chastity. The Jewish Mishnah states that wearing the hair uncovered can be a sign of being a loose woman and be grounds for divorce. Jewish men say that the hair is sensually and sexually arousing.

Online photos show three primary head-covering styles worn by Orthodox Jewish women on city streets and when in Judaism's holiest sites—the snood, fall, and hat. Most married Orthodox women cover their heads, usually with hair wigs.

In Conservative and Reform communities, most women do not

cover their hair on a daily basis, although in synagogue congregations some women do during prayer as a sign of respect for God, just like men cover their heads. A 1990 Reform statement says, "We Reform Jews object vigorously to this requirement for women, which places them in an inferior position and sees them primarily in a sexual role."

The Stories That Jewish Hats Tell

The yarmulke or *kippah*, also spelled as is a kipah/kipa/kippa brimless cap, usually made of cloth or crocheted yarn, worn traditionally by Jewish males to meet the Bible's requirement that the head be covered. Men and boys in Orthodox communities wear it at all times. Males (and some females) in non-Orthodox communities typically wear them only during prayer or rituals. Most synagogues and sites like Yad Vashem (the Holocaust Museum), the Western Wall, etc., require males to wear them and usually keep some on hand, sometimes made of paper, to supply those who arrive without them.

How do men and boys keep the yarmulkes or kippahs on? Very carefully! They often use a well-placed hair clip at the back of the yarmulke. I have seen these flap in the breeze or fly off the wearer's head before they quickly scurry to retrieve them.

Orthodox Jewish fathers wear long black coats and black hats.

Those of Russian background wear large round fur hats. Both groups wear bouncing ear locks. One rabbi held a young daughter by each hand as all three happily skipped down a narrow Old City street unashamed. A young boy, maybe age ten, dressed in his black hat and long coat rushed through the Old City to the larger outer city with a skateboard over each shoulder. I would have loved to see him ride.

A shtreimel is a fur hat worn by married Orthodox Jewish men on Shabbat, Jewish holidays, or other festive occasions, particularly (but not limited to) members of Hasidic Judaism to demonstrate strict adherence to their understanding of Jewish law.

Tefillin (also called phylacteries) are black leather boxes with leather straps that Orthodox Jewish men wear on their forehead and right arm (near their heart) during weekday morning prayer, sabbath/shabbat, and on other special occasions. Observant Jews consider wearing tefillin to be a very important command (mitzvah).

A mezuzah is a scroll-shaped decorative container holding a parchment with specific Hebrew Torah verses. It is attached to the doorposts of Jewish homes to fulfill the Bible command to "write the words of God on the gates and doorposts of your house" (Deuteronomy 6:9).

A menorah is the seven-lamp (six branched) lampstand like that made of pure beaten gold described in scripture for dedicated use in the tabernacle by Moses in the wilderness and later in Solomon's Temple in Jerusalem.

## Israel's Governing Bodies

**The Knesset** is Israel's unicameral House of Representatives with 120 members elected in national elections every four years. Its name comes from the Hebrew phrase for Great Assembly, "Knesset HaGedola," which convened in Jerusalem after the Jews returned from Babylonian exile in the fifth century BC/BCE. It was then an assembly of 120 scribes, sages, and prophets until the rise of Rabbinic Judaism around 200 BC/BCE.

The Knesset buildings are near the Israeli Museum and the Shrine of the Book. The latter houses The Dead Sea Scrolls. Discovered in 1946, but purchased in 1948, Israel's year of statehood, they confirm scriptures and are safeguarded as a national treasure. Many also see them as a property deed confirming God's gift of the land to the Jewish people to live in and steward.

Early Israel was a Kritarchy ruled by Judges before the people demanded a king to be like the other nations around them. After the people suffered the Babylonian captivity and returned, they were governed by a theocratic body called the Sanhedrin. It was a supreme council tribunal for the Jewish people during post-exilic times headed by a High Priest with religious, civil, and criminal jurisdiction. That three-part prophet, priest, and king system corresponds to the balanced triumvirate of legislative, judicial, and executive branches established for the US Government in our Constitution. However, Israel follows the Parliamentary form of governing.

Today, Israel is considered the most democratic nation in the Middle East with elected leaders, but there is also talk of recreating the religious Sanhedrin to oversee the building of the Third Temple.

Some historians think that the Dome of the Rock occupies the exact location on the Temple Mount where the previous temples were built. They expect the Third Temple to be built on that site as well but say the previous temples were likely located closer to the Al Aksa Mosque. Today, between Jews and Muslims, the Temple Mount may be the world's most hotly contested piece of real estate.

If there is turmoil on the Temple Mount near the Western Wall, it most often occurs on Fridays (Sabbaths). I avoid going there on that day. If I need to be in the area, the staff in Christ Church Coffee Shop two blocks inside Jaffa Gate and next to the post office usually knows what's happening and carries morning newspapers with reliable reports.

Israel has secular and religious courts for those of the Jewish faith. They are rabbinic with judges selected by a committee headed by the Minister of Justice. There are twelve regional rabbinic courts, a special conversion court, and the Great Rabbinical Court, chaired by one of Israel's two Chief Rabbis. Since the Chief Rabbinate is governed by Ultra-Orthodox sects, the Reform and Conservative groups don't feel equally represented. There is a struggle in Orthodox circles to allow more rabbis to perform marriages and permit alternative views. Marriages and divorces of Jewish couples are recently only handled by rabbinical decree, although issues involving custody, support, or property division are determined by civil courts.

Along with full access to civil courts, Israeli citizens also have access to Muslim and Druze religious courts for adherents of those faiths. Religious Sharia law based on the Quran is the governing system Islamic followers establish where they have authority.

Those govern all aspects of society from how women are to dress to how states are run.

Languages

**Hebrew** is an ancient Northwestern Semitic language closely related to Phoenician and Moabite. Scholars often place them both in a Canaanite subgroup. The western dialect of Aramaic supplanted Hebrew in the 3rd century BC, although Hebrew continued being used in liturgy and literature. Hebrew is the ancient language of the Israelites and their ancestors and today is spoken by over nine million people worldwide. It was revived in spoken form in the 19th and 20th centuries and remains Israel's official language today.

**The Hebrew Bible,** also called the *Tanakh* or *Mikra*, is the canonical collection of Hebrew Scriptures, including the Torah (the first five books of the Bible written by Moses). These texts are almost exclusively in biblical Hebrew, except for a few passages in biblical Aramaic.

**Yiddish** is the historical language used by Ashkenazi Jews in Central and Eastern Europe before the Holocaust. Originally a German dialect, it developed in the 9th century AD/CE with influence from Hebrew, Aramaic, and Romance languages. It remains spoken in Russia, Israel, and the United States. For example, "It tastes good" in German is, "Es schmeckt gut," but in Yiddish it is expressed, "Es teysts gut." Its 1.5 million speakers live primarily in Western, Central, and Eastern Europe. In Israel, it is spoken mostly by the ultra-Orthodox. It is an old language that is slowly dying away.

The Jewish and Arab people are cousins with closely related languages. Shalom is the Hebrew word meaning "peace" that Jewish people use in greeting or parting. "Salaam" carries that same meaning in Arabic. In Hebrew, *todah* (sometimes *towdah*) means "thank you." "*Todah rabah*" means "thank you very much" or "great thanks"—actually, "a heart full of thanks." Its Arabic equivalent, *shukran*, is usually said twice. I enjoy connecting with local people anywhere, so work hard to remember such phrases. I find being able to express thanks in Hebrew and Arabic contributes to meaningful cooperation and relationships.

Here's one highlight of the first trip to Israel when Cindy and I stayed at Moshe and Tina's. They trusted us to stay in their home while they had to be away for the weekend. Friday sabbath/shabbat arrived and shops closed at noon. Food was in the refrigerator, but we wanted more groceries. I stopped on the building's ground floor at a small branch of the Super-Sol supermarket chain, while Cindy headed home to begin cooking. I bought eggs and milk, and we wanted the delicious special braided challah bread Israelis eat on Sabbaths and ceremonial days. I didn't see it displayed so I asked the proprietor. He spoke no English. I'd had four years of French and baby level Spanish but knew few Hebrew words. I gestured and did charades, but nothing worked. Then I remembered, "Bethlehem" means "house of bread" in Hebrew. Beth is "house" so "*lechem*" means "*bread.*" "*Lechem, lechem*" I said in probably the worst accent ever.

He nodded, repeating, "*lechem, lechem,*" and stepped into the back room. He came back with a beautiful loaf of fresh braided challah. We enjoyed that bread all weekend, but I was happiest at successfully communicating when neither the shopkeeper nor I knew the other's language.

I could write a book about how on the 2019 trip our rented GPS took us to places we didn't intend to go, but I'll keep it to one story. Several times during our day in Abu Ghosh when we asked our GPS to take us to a well-known site, it led us instead down narrow stone-walled alleys. The first was a dead end. Back-up driving is not my forté anywhere, let alone in foreign counties as an onlooking Arab grandfather observed. He hid a smile while giving hand signals to show how close I came to the stone wall on either side of the narrow lane or when I needed to straighten my wheels. I told him shukran often.

Later, I needed similar help from an Arab woman in modern dress as I entered her walled driveway to back up and turn around. In perfect American English she blurted out, "You speak Arabic?"

"No. Just shukran, shukran," I said.

Next, our navigation device directed us down a passageway barely wide enough for a single car, except another vehicle was advancing toward us from the bottom of the hill.

"Disaster," I groaned, picturing our rental with costly dents and scrapes I would pay for. The oncoming driver, a woman in full black Arab dress and head covering, saw my dilemma and backed down the lane a full block and a half to allow my escape. "Shukran, shukran," I said with feeling as I inched past to freedom, broadly smiling all the thanks in my heart. At the exact moment we faced each other, our car windows open, that lovely stranger kissed her fingertips, waved them at me, and winked. I value that moment.

Driving crises are embarrassing. Worse, they sometimes lead to road rage, potentially even more when different people groups and nations are involved. But after that day's events, I felt like I had met those individuals. We had exchanged pleasantries. We assisted and liked each other. That encounter made me think improved world peace might be possible when people actually meet and spend time together.

Thankfully, no car damage was sustained in the incident just described. I won't reveal details of the super-glue bumper fix a friend helped me do in Jerusalem which saved me considerable rental car damage fees. On another occasion, a bit of matching paint proved more important than glue. Comprehensive car insurance protection is expensive in Israel.

I'm actually glad for that GPS misdirection. We learned from the tough challenges of unfamiliar narrow roadways requiring stellar attitudes, committed teamwork, and problem-solving by the brave souls riding with me. In that process, we exchanged kind words and frequent smiles with strangers. My only photos of those events are in my heart which filled with thanksgiving. I believe theirs did, too.

The concept of gratitude is basic and central to Judaism. The word "Jew" comes from "Judah," also a form of the Hebrew word that means "thank you." We are to be grateful in all things at all times. In fact, faithful Jews are to say a minimum of one hundred blessings of thanks every day. That would be good practice for all of us, no matter our racial or religious heritage.

I believe that the same deep far-reaching attitude of gratitude is also central in the culture and hearts of Arabic friends. Each time I take people to Israel with me, I provide a list of helpful phrases that lets them ask questions and master simple statements. At first my list was English and Hebrew only. It is now expanded to include Arabic. While most people in Israel speak and understand English, it is always good to know basic phrases for use in the language of any country being visited. In addition, inhabitants appreciate our efforts to reach out and communicate with them.

At the end of the book, I've included a chart of useful English/Hebrew/Arabic phrases used in Israel.

**Weather, Clothing, Electronics and Main Products**

### Weather

When planning a travel schedule, save outdoor activities for good weather days and indoor sights for less ideal times. Israel's weather is amazing, but any place has imperfect days. Weather reports are available on any internet search engine by entering the desired location plus "weather."

### Clothing tips–layer and dress to fit in

Light-weight clothing pieces in mix or match colors worn in layers are great answers for any climate and simplify packing. Even hot nations like Israel, Spain, and the Philippines have cool mornings and evenings when sweaters or light jackets are welcome. When storms or high winds roll in, lightweight roll-up plastic raincoats or ponchos weigh almost nothing, cost little, and save the day. It is better to bring and not use them than to need them but not have them along.

Some destinations are windy. Folding fabric or plastic rain hats give ear protection besides keeping heads dry. I get earaches from high winds or intense cold AC blasts, so I bring lightweight Swix earmuffs with me. They fit fine under scarves, hats, or bike helmets, and are hardly noticeable. But even if they were visible, comfort trumps appearance. I've worn them on Philippine buses when fierce direct A/C brought severe ear pain. I hoped the other passengers would think my mini-earmuffs were the newest style of North American headphones.

Comfortable walking shoes are also essential. Again, comfort trumps beauty. If suitcase space permits, bring an extra pair or two of additional favorite lightweight shoes for variety or dress-up. Or buy new shoes in the country visited. Israel is famous for manufacturing high-quality sandals that travelers love to buy, use there, and bring home.

In the Smart Safety Tips section, I include proven ideas Tina Goldenberg shared for how to enjoy the culture and fit in like a local instead of sticking out like a foreigner. I avoid popular wornat-the-waist traveler's fanny packs, especially after talking with one tourist who was robbed near Rome when thieves slashed the belt to steal hers. I prefer carrying a local shopping bag on my shoulder like an area housewife buying groceries. In that bag, I have my wallet, iPhone, sometimes my passport, and perhaps my tape recorder turned on to record things like Muslim calls to prayer in sensitive areas where obvious recording might not be appreciated. I avoid clothing or bags with trendy North American university, designer, or sports logos. It's fun blending in, although I'm told that our nationality can be revealed by our consistently high-quality North American shoes.

(Note: A savvy Spanish friend and I were riding a crowded train near Madrid. She carried a stylish purse that opened via a magnetic flap. Although Gracia is a careful, experienced traveler, while we were being jostled in the train aisle, someone pushed up her purse's flap and stole her billfold, ID, credit cards, and four hundred Euros. She bought a replacement purse that did not open easily, but it was a bitter and expensive lesson learned.)

**Electronics and Communication Systems and Methods**

Electrical adapters are required for travel outside of North America so that U.S. plugs can fit the local wall sockets. Like Europe,

Israel is on 220V, but their power plug prongs and three-hole pattern are unique. Sometimes European "round" prongs fit but not always. Converters for European or American prongs are sold at most hardware or electrical stores in Israel at low cost.

However, to simplify things, I recommend purchasing a worldwide Universal Travel Adapter that works everywhere. I have owned two and been pleased with both. (Note: Don't leave an adapter plugged in and charging if you get up extra early to leave in the morning as you may accidentally leave it behind, which is why I've owned two.) Check helpful online links like How to choose Travel Power Adapters for individual nations or continents at https://www.rei.com/learn/expert-advice/world-electricity-guide.html

**Phones**—In years past, we were told it was not a good idea to purchase cell phones in Israel. On our 2023 trip, one on our team needed to buy a new phone in Jerusalem, and all went well. It's also easy to buy SIM cards.

On our 2018 trip, eight of us in two cars communicated by phone. For our first two days in Tel Aviv/Joppa/Jaffa/Yafo after arrival, much was within walking distance of our hostel, so we didn't collect our second rental car until the morning of Day Three when we were ready to head north. The driver of our first car dropped a friend and me at Ben Gurion to get the second rental vehicle. It helped having someone ride shotgun in this second car to help with phone connection and to navigate in heavy traffic. Abraham Hostel downtown was hard to find because of the city's many curved narrow one-way streets. My friend, Pat, came with me but developed worsening laryngitis. The more she tried to talk to our other driver on the phone, the less voice she had until she had none.

"What?" Mike said. "I can't hear you."

After Pat tried again but only squeaked with no sound, she handed me her phone.

"We're on HaRakevet close to Levontin," I told Mike an instant before a police car's revolving light flashed and its siren alerted us to pull over. It was hard to find space to do so on the narrow street.

"What's the problem," I asked.

"Do they let you talk on phones and drive in England?" The officer glared.

"I'm not from England, but it's legal where I live in the United States."

"Not in Tel Aviv. I could take your license, even your rental car, and put you in jail."

He pulled out his ticket pad.

Pat leaned over, trying to explain, but couldn't speak.

I told the officer I only took the phone when her voice failed, and we had to contact our other car. The officer let us go after his serious warning, but I haven't talked on a phone in Israel while driving again. Instead, I pull over or find other solutions. I share this to help others avoid our scare.

**Israel's Exports and Imports**

Each traveler compiles their own favorite list, but certain product specialties are associated with each nation. Exquisite lead crystal or lace from Ireland. Oat cakes, fabulous jams and jellies, and woolens and tartans from Scotland. Jewel-grade amber, glassware, and modern furniture designs from Denmark. Cheeses, spring bulbs, and wooden shoes from the Netherlands. We know France's pommes frites as world-famous French fries. Visitors love artisan cheeses from Switzerland plus chocolates, Swiss Army Knives, and edelweiss-themed patterns. Belgium has world-famous chocolates and handmade lace. There are endless wonderful goods from many unique places.

Israel excels in natural and manufactured exports. Besides producing possibly the finest sandals in the world, they offer wonderful fresh dates, spices, electronics, ancient artifacts, original art, ceramics, handwoven rugs and textiles, olive wood carvings, cashmere scarves, Roman glass, Yemenite and a wide variety of ethnic jewelry—the list is endless and impressive.

**Things to Do**

- Do use local terms and phrases in the right circumstances but be aware of your surroundings. Citizens of other countries appreciate our efforts to learn their language and connect with nations and people.
- Do be in tune with the areas you're visiting. As much as possible, be aware of local holidays, public events, or of rare civil strife or public protests. When we were in Israel during the time of Yasser Arafat's passing, extra precautions were in place including the Old City being closed due to unrest, but the public was constantly kept well-informed.
- Do practice cultural sensitivity. If you wish to photograph people or sensitive places, ask permission. It will usually be granted. Sometimes you may be asked to pay something to photograph a camel or a particularly interesting scene or location.
- Do represent your nation and values well. While traveling, our attitudes, conduct, and interactions with the nation's people should represent the best of our values back home. Travelers truly represent far more than ourselves.

**Things Not to Do**

- Do not think accident or sickness cannot happen to you. Inquiry may prove that your state or national medical insurance coverage applies in foreign countries. I'm told mine does but haven't had to test it. Not having a policy or plan in place may invite disaster.
- Do not take shortcuts unless you know the area. As a freespirited North American woman, I like short cuts. They may work at home but are not always wise in foreign countries.

On the trip to Israel when my son, Aaron, joined me, we were on the Temple Mount on a Friday around noon heading for St. Stephen's Gate when we saw activity in a courtyard bordering the Temple Mount. We hesitantly walked forward, knowing this was a Moslem enclave, though shopkeepers and hawkers were still marketing wares. As we approached the next archway, men inside were sitting on the pavement in rows in white robes with their shoes off and piled in a heap on the floor in front of them. I didn't realize that this open paved area was the beginning of the Mosque of Omar or the Dome of the Rock. When a prominent man in the front row waved us off in a mild manner, we gladly left and passed through St. Stephen's Gate and down the Kedron Valley to the Mount of Olives. Hordes of poor Moslems coming to the mosque passed by us. One boy with a tray of Arab breadsticks balanced on his head dropped the whole load and nonchalantly picked them up and dusted them off again before continuing on his way.

On another Friday on my first trip in Israel when Cindy accompanied me, we started a shortcut from Damascus Gate to the Via Dolorosa. Many small pamphlets printed in Arabic littered the ground. The Grand Ayatollah Khomeini, Iran's first Islamic cleric, had just died. The area around Damascus Gate seemed deserted and strangely quietly until we entered and a young man appeared and asked, "Where are you going?"

When I told him, he said, "You don't want to go that way today."

I showed him my map. "Doesn't this route connect if we go straight?"

"Yes, but you don't want to go that way today," he repeated.

Then I understood his meaning and thanked him for his help.

Whatever was happening further inside the Quarter, it was best that two unescorted western women not walk through alone.

I learned to carefully consider Friday schedules. It is generally a good day to avoid being in the Old City except for perhaps staying in the Jaffa Gate Christian Quarter. Fridays are the days when Muslims travel the Old City's narrow streets around noon following prayers.

Jewish Quarter stores close early on Fridays allowing their residents to prepare for Shabbat.

## Dee's Insider Savings Tips

- Most car rental companies occasionally offer sales or discount coupons. Take time to compare.
- Remember, fuel costs in Israel are high, about double of those in the U.S. Pay attention to fuel consumption ratings when selecting a rental vehicle.
- One jewelry store in the Jewish Quarter previously gave free maps of the Old City. They did not do so when we were there in November 2019, but it's worth buying an Old City map to find direct walking routes through the fascinating narrow twisting streets to save steps and time. Nearly all shopkeepers speak English and are also helpful in clarifying directions as needed.
- The majority of shopkeepers are honest and charge fair prices. However, when shopping anywhere, it's wise to compare items in several places before purchasing. You'll quickly get a sense of which businesses and shopkeepers are the most friendly and helpful. If they have time, shopkeepers enjoy talking with visitors. Feel free to ask their recommendations to locate the items you're looking for if they do not sell them.

On one occasion, when I bought a pottery bowl in a shop in the Armenian Quarter, I noticed one in the display was cracked. The salesman offered to wrap my purchase in newspaper as they often do. I noticed the cracked bowl was now gone from the pile and thought I'd better check my package. When I partially opened it, I saw the cracked item. The shopkeeper gasped, saying, "How did that get in there?" He made the situation right and exchanged the item, but I'm glad I looked.

There's one shop near Jaffa Gate that offers good prices on featured items in the entry way to get you into the store. Inside, they primarily sell jewelry. Prices start reasonably but then the salesmen talk faster and faster and the final cost can be exorbitant. I returned the next day with one team member who needed to return an exorbitantly priced item for refund or have the final price corrected. The shopkeeper pointed out that in small print the receipt said, "No returns allowed." After lengthy discussion, we did prevail and got a significant amount of the cost refunded. Poor business practice is rare in Israel but stay alert. Shopkeepers anywhere can be tempted to exploit buyers.

# 3

# USEFUL KNOWLEDGE

**Israel's People and Primary Religions**

There are few nations, if any, who can say they were formed by God over 3,000 years ago. His covenant promises to Abraham are the basis of Israel's existence as a nation. The Lord formed Israel; they are His people. It's traced back to Genesis 12 where God told Abraham, "I will make of thee a great nation, and I will bless thee, and make thy name great; and thou shalt be a blessing: And I will bless them that bless thee, and curse him that curseth thee: and in thee shall all families of the earth be blessed."

**Israel's people are one nation—two people.** Israel's two primary people groups are cousins. Abraham is the patriarch father of both the Arabs and the Jews. Many of the same prophets are honored in both religions.

For centuries, Palestine was an annexed province of the Ottoman Empire. The United Nations presently defines it as an entity with non-state status claiming the West Bank of the Jordan River bordering and Israel Jordan plus the Gaza Strip.

After World War II, the UN adopted a Partition Plan for what had been British Mandate Palestine. They recommended creating independent Arab and Jewish states with Jerusalem as an international city. However, the Arab states rejected the Partition Plan. When the UN approved a Jewish State of Israel in May 1948, Arab armies invaded.

Leon Uris's novel, *Exodus,* describes the steps of modern Israel's settlement and birth. The book became a blockbuster movie and its theme song, "This Land Is Mine," won best Soundtrack Album and Song in the 1960 Academy Awards.

In 1967, when Jordan attacked Israel in the Six Day War, Israel captured Judea and Samaria, Israel's Heartland, which Arabs call the West Bank. Jewish people saw this as a great victory as ancient biblical Jerusalem, Judea, and Samaria returned to Jewish sovereignty. Part of the region is Palestinian-run with its own security force, but Israel is the ultimate governing authority.

Later, Syria also attacked Israel, resulting in Israel regaining the Golan Heights, formerly biblical Bashan settled by the tribe of Manasseh.

In 1988, Yasser Arafat declared the creation of a Palestinian state and the Palestine Liberation Organization (PLO) terrorist organization.

In 1994, after signing the Oslo Accords, Arafat moved from Tunisia to Ramallah and created the Palestinian National Authority to govern parts of the West Bank and Gaza Strip. Another terrorist organization, Hamas, overran Palestinian control of Gaza in 2007.

The "State of Palestine" is recognized by eight of one hundred and ninety-three UN member nations and operates with non-member observer status.

Car license plates show residency at a glance. Palestinian plates are green or white. Israel's are yellow. Travelers enter the Palestinian territories by passing through Israel Defense Force (IDF) checkpoints.

Israel's Arabs are usually bilingual with their second language being modern Hebrew. Most are Muslim, usually the Sunni branch of Islam. There is also a small active Arab Christian minority.

Druze practitioners in northern Israel are said to follow a unique variation of Islam. George Clooney's wife, Amal, is of Lebanese Druze heritage.

According to Israel's Central Bureau of Statistics, Muslims, including Bedouins, are 82% of the nation's Arab population along with 9% Druze, and 9% Christian Arabs. Predictions say that Israel's Arabs will reach 25% of the population by 2025. Most live in Arab-majority towns or cities and attend separate schools. Some are Israeli citizens but many retain Jordanian citizenship and decline Israeli citizenship.

The village of Abu Ghosh west of Jerusalem is a success story with a prosperous Arab population. The village represents Jews, Christians, and Arabs living peacefully and closely together. There are also prosperous Arab towns in the Galilee.

Bedouin means nomadic Arab people who are desert dwellers. Israel's Foreign Affairs Minister reports that 110,000 Bedouins live in the Negev, 50,000 in the Galilee, and 10,000 in Central Israel.

Before Israel's statehood, 65,000–90,000 Bedouin lived in the Negev. Israel's government relocated them to a ten per cent area of the northeastern Negev where seven development towns were established and where half of the Bedouin population now lives.

## Israel's Main Religions–Judaism, Christianity, Islam, Baha'i, and Druze

### Judaism's Major sites

Judaism is the world's oldest monotheistic religion with an oral and written history reaching back nearly four-thousand years and containing religious, cultural, and legal teachings. Today the world's Jewish population is nearly fifteen million people. Jewish people currently account for 1.8% of the world's population. However, throughout history, God has blessed them and made them a blessing to all people as promised in Genesis 12. Through ideas, inventions, and breakthroughs they are among the world's most influential contributors in many fields. They represent twenty percent of all Nobel Prize winners.

Israel's Bureau of Statistics reports that 8% of Israel's Jewish population identifies itself as Ultra-Orthodox, 12% as Orthodox, 13% as traditional-religious, 25% as traditional, and 42% as secular or cultural Jews only.

Old Testament scriptures required the Jewish people to go up to Jerusalem three times each year to observe and celebrate the three major feasts. (The faithful still do, and traffic during those times is horrendous. That's why I needed a super-glue bumper fix.)

Israel's King David penned around fifty of the Bible's one hundred and fifty Psalms. Fifteen of them, those numbering 120– 134 (or 119–133 in the Septuagint and Vulgate), are titled "Songs of Ascents" or degrees to be sung by faithful pilgrims coming from all parts of Israel to ascend the hills to Jerusalem and Mount Zion. They sang these Psalms to review and prepare their hearts while approaching Judaism's holiest place of worship, the Temple.

Pesach (Passover), Shavuot (Feast of Weeks or Pentecost), and Sukkot (Tabernacles, Tents or Booths) were discussed earlier.

Religious governing bodies in Israel control many things, including immigration, citizenship, marriages, divorces, etc. Israel's Chief Rabbi has control over Jewish marriages. He also has the right to refuse someone the status of being recognized as a Jew, complicating legal union in Israel.

In addition, the Rabbinate and local religious councils are the only ones able to register rabbis to perform weddings. Rabbinic control also means that many of the 400,000 Russians who have moved to Israel are not considered halachically Jewish (according to rabbinic law.) Therefore, they are not permitted to marry in Israel, forcing many to travel outside of the country to wed.

The conflict for land ownership between Israelis and Arabs includes the fierce battle over Jerusalem and its Old City, home to sites holy to Jews, Muslims, and Christians. Jerusalem's "New City" flourishes beyond the Old City's walls.

Most Jewish sites also hold significance to followers of

Christianity and Islam. Sites along the Sea of Galilee are strongly connected to the life and ministry of Jesus so have profound meaning especially for Christians.

**Christianity's Major Sites**

The majority of travelers to Israel are familiar with Christianity, so I will describe its major sites but not discuss its beliefs.

**Abu-Ghosh, Emmaus**—The Benedictine monastery, St. Mary of the Resurrection Abbey, is run by the Olivetan Benedictine order. It is centered on the Church of the Resurrection, or Church of our Lord's Resurrection, built by 12th century crusaders above Roman ruins in the center of Abu Ghosh. Crusaders assumed that the village, which they called Fontenoid and the Arabs called Qaryet al-'Inab until the 19th century, stood at the site of Emmaus according to Luke's gospel. France claimed ownership of the monastery's land under Ottoman terms formalized by the Fischer-Chauvel Agreement of 1948 but not ratified by Israel.

**The Ark of the Covenant**—Also at Abu Ghosh, Our Lady of the Ark of the Covenant Church is crowned with a statue of Mary carrying the infant Jesus. This hilltop church, built on the site of Kiryat Ya'arim, is believed by many to be where the Ark of the Covenant remained during the reigns of Kings Samuel, Saul, and David. A 5th-century mosaic visible on the church floor is preserved from the earlier Byzantine basilica that has been destroyed and rebuilt many times. In 1924, the Knights Hospitaller founded another church 400 meters east of the Church of Our Lady of the Ark of the Covenant. According to tradition, this structure takes the place of the house of Abinadab where the Ark of the Covenant rested for twenty years until King David captured Jerusalem. That church was built on the site of a fifth-century Byzantine church.

Many Christians take communion on the hill overlooking the town. Some think that the glory that rested with the Ark of the Covenant for three months in that place is the cause of today's blessings.

**Ein Kerem** (sometimes Ein Karem)–the Church of the Nativity of St. John the Baptist with notable mosaics marks the traditional birthplace of John the Baptist, the son born to Zachariah and Elizabeth in their old age, who announced the coming of his cousin, Jesus Christ. The picturesque village is 4.7 miles or 7.5 km southwest of Jerusalem. The Gospel of Luke, chapter 1 describes the angel Gabriel, appearing to the aged priest as he served in the Temple to announce that his wife, Elizabeth, would bear a son. Because Zechariah was skeptical, he was struck dumb until his son was born. In the meantime, Gabriel also appeared to the teenage virgin, Mary, in Nazareth, telling her that she would become the mother of Jesus and revealed that her elderly cousin, Elizabeth, was six months pregnant. Mary "went with haste to the Judean town in the hill country—" nearly 75 miles or 120 km.

When she entered the home of Zechariah and greeted her cousin, "the child leaped in Elizabeth's womb" (Luke 1:39-41). Mary's Well in the town is thought to be near where this scriptural reference took place.

**Latrun** is a Cistercian Abbey near the Latrun Interchange where Highway 1 and Highway 3 intersect. Founded in 1890, its name derives from a crusader castle once there. The abbey's Guest Master interacts with visitors, but its Trappist monks practice silence. Besides religious duties, they produce quality cheeses for sale. The thriving community of monks offers silent and non-silent retreats to those desiring them.

**Yardenit** is a beautiful baptismal site where the Jordan River leaves the Sea of Galilee representing the place where John the Baptist baptized Jesus. According to tradition, the actual location was Qasr al-Yahud further south near Jericho and the Dead Sea which could not be accessed because of minefields until 2011.

**Yahud-Qasr al** is believed to be the actual site on the Jordan River five miles (nine km.) east of Jericho and an equal distance north of the Dead Sea where John the Baptist baptized Jesus. It is also identified as the place where the Israelites crossed the Jordan to enter the Promised Land and where Elijah ascended to heaven in a fiery chariot after parting the river for him and Elisha to cross over. Now cleared of mines and administered by Israel's Nature and Parks Authority, it is open to the public free of charge. A rope with floats bisects the narrow Jordan River as the official boundary dividing Israel from The Kingdom of Jordan. Christians descend steps for baptism on both sides of the river. Believers from both nations stand feet apart. Beautiful songs rise from both groups. In 2021, the site celebrated the removal of all remaining mines.

## Islam

Islam is the world's second largest religion. Its roots draw from Jewish and Christian influences further developed by the prophet Muhammad. Its origin is traced to the 7th century AD/CE, making it the world's youngest major world religion.

Muslims pray five times a day—at sunrise, midday, during the afternoon, shortly after sunset, and at dark. Praying is done at home, at work, or wherever the person is. Those praying prostrate themselves on a prayer mat and use a special cap or head cover.

Mosque attendance is required on Fridays at midday when adult males are expected to attend. In Israel, the Muslim call to prayer is heard over loudspeakers. In 2023, Islam's followers number 2.01 billion or 24% of the world's population, making it the second largest religion after Christianity.

**Israel's important Islamic sites:**

**The Dome of the Rock** built in Jerusalem in 687 AD/CE, fiftyfive years after Muhammad's death, is not a mosque but a shrine for prayers with magnificent architecture. It commemorates the Muslim belief of Muhammad's ascent into heaven and is the third holiest site in Islam after Mecca and Medina.

**The Al-Aqsa *Mosque*** stands in the Old City on the far southern side of the Temple Mount facing Mecca. Built on the Temple Mount, called the Al Aqsa Compound or Haram esh-Sharif, it is several hundred yards from the Dome of the Rock. Muslims believe that Muhammad was transported from Mecca's Great Mosque to al-Aqsa during his Night Journey.

**The Ayyubid Mosque of Omar**, built in 1193 AD/CE by Saladin near the Dome of the Rock, stands opposite the southern courtyard of the Church of the Holy Sepulcher. The sign at its door says it is available for prayers only. The name Jerusalem does not appear in the *Quran*.

**The Mosque of Omar in Bethlehem** is named for Omar Khattab-ibn al (Umar), the second Rashidun Muslim Caliph. A Christian monk there advised him to build a mosque adjacent to the Church of the Nativity rather than transforming that church into a mosque.

**The Baha'i Faith** is a religion birthed in Iran in the mid-19th century blending Jewish, Christian, and Islamic faiths. It teaches the value and equality of all people. They have developed the Baha'i Gardens, world-famous terraced floral gardens, one of Israel's most visited sites.

**The Druze Religion** is an Arabic-speaking ethnoreligious group developed in 986 AD/CE as a movement within Islam. They regard Jethro of Midian as their spiritual founder and chief prophet. Around 143,000 live in settlements in northern Israel with 250,000 in nearby Lebanon. One skill they are known for is distinctive, beautifully colored embroideries and tapestries. I was pleased to buy several.

## Government System and Statistics

The Prime Minister is the government head appointed by the majority coalition of seats. Like the Knesset, the government serves for four years unless its term is shortened by resignation, incapacitation, the death of the prime minister, or a Knesset nonconfidence vote.

As the nation's ninth Prime Minister, Benjamin Netanyahu ruled longer than any other elected Prime Minister in Israel's history. Despite varying opinions regarding his leadership, he was known to keep an Old Testament on his desk and held Bible studies in his office. Before Israel's 70th anniversary, he scheduled assigned scripture reading portions so that Israelis could read through the Old Testament during a two-year period to complete Malachi on May 14, 2018, Israel's seventieth anniversary as a nation.

In May 2020, after several elections failed to seat a majority, a shared government was formed with Benny Gantz as a co-prime minister who would later succeed Netanyahu and head his own government. However, that also failed due to Covid and other health and economic crises.

A fourth national election in March 2021 did establish an outcome, and on June 13, 2021, Naftali Bennett was sworn in as Israel's 13th prime minister. However, his administration failed to win a confidence vote and was dissolved that month with the next election held in the fall of 2022. Then Benjamin Netanyahu was reelected with a more conservative right-wing coalition than expected. The country deserves governmental and economic stability no matter who is in power. Starting in January 2023, protesters have been staging large anti-government protests, especially in Tel Aviv, regarding proposed reforms to reduce the judicial powers of the Supreme Court. The tensions and size of the protests are increasing at the time of this writing. The nation's coalition remains fragile and in flux.

According to Jewish Virtual League Vital Statistics, as of December 2019, Israel was home to 6.8 million Jews (42.1% of world and 74.1% of Israel's Jewish population), while the U.S. is home to 5.7 million or 39%. Israel's Arab population is 1,900,000 or 21% of Israel's current population. Christians, Bahai, and nonArabs make up the remaining 5% of the population.

Besides the growing numbers of annual visitors during non-C variant times, Israel has a high number of Jewish immigrants making Aliyah, the biblical homecoming of people of Jewish origin to return to the land. This last decade has been Israel's highest rate of return so far, with 2019 receiving over 3,000 immigrants, large numbers coming from Russia and France. Immigration and citizenship application is based on proven Jewish heritage but is complicated and can be denied if Christian involvement is evident.

**Ashkelon/Ashqelon/or Ascalon** is a coastal city in Israel's Southern District. Located 12 miles north of Gaza, along the Mediterranean coast, ancient Tel Ashkelon was a powerful city for thousands of years, built and rebuilt under Canaanites, Philistines, and Romans. Now, a project is underway to present the archaeological remains of this impressive site in a manner fitting its former glory. A major goal is to restore the site's Roman basilica and Odeon.

**Things to Do**

- Do use local terms and phrases in the right circumstances but be aware of your surroundings. Citizens of other countries appreciate our efforts to connect with nations and people.
- Request permission to take photos of individuals or private settings. For example, even if travelers appreciate seeing a camel but are not paying for a ride, they may be asked to give something, although it is not always necessary. This can usually be determined by pleasant discussion.

**Things Not to Do**

- Do not practice speaking a language in the wrong place. My son, Aaron, has a gift for learning foreign languages. When traveling with me, I jabbed him in the ribs each time he accidentally began practicing speaking Hebrew in an Arabic-speaking shop. When visiting places of interest in Jerusalem's Old City Muslim Quarter and asked to sign in, instead of writing his given name, Aaron, which is distinctively Jewish and Christian, he signed Charlie McGillicutty.

- Do not take photos or record private situations without asking permission.
- Do not act like the privileged North Americans presented in William Lederer's 1958 book, *The Ugly American*, describing occasionally arrogant, entitled American conduct abroad. Nothing pleases me more than having Jewish and Arab Israelis single out my teams and me to thank us for coming and supporting the country.

**Dee's Insider Savings Tips**

- Once you've selected your desired destinations, check to see if certain days or times offer free admissions.
- Remember, National Parks and other locations offer generous frequent visitor discounts. Plan accordingly.
- Many places in Israel extend senior and/or professional discounts to citizens and often to visitors as well. Ask to see if you qualify.

# 4

# THINGS TO SEE AND DO

**Israel's Geography and Major Destinations**

Understanding Israel's geography will help you schedule and plan well. This nation is the hub connecting Europe, Asia, and Africa, influencing history, trade, religion, philosophy, inventions, and much in world history. It includes varied climates, terrain, and scenery in one compact area. Their latitude and longitude give it a Mediterranean coast climate and vegetation comparable to California or European Mediterranean nations.

Israel's climate ranges from burning desert in the south to snow-capped mountains in the north. The Mediterranean Sea and the smaller Gaza Strip make up Israel's 170-mile (273 km.) coastline. Israel shares its northern border with Lebanon, its northeastern with Syria, its eastern with Jordan and Judea-Samaria or the West Bank (of the Jordan River), and its southwestern with Egypt plus a small coastline on the Red Sea. In addition, tourists often travel into the Sinai to climb Mt. Sinai or to explore desert areas.

The Gaza Strip, part of Gaza, is on the Mediterranean's eastern edge bordering Egypt on the southwest for 6.8 miles (11 km.) and Israel on the east and north along a 32 mile (51 km.) border. Separate from the Palestinian territories, it is presently governed by Hamas, the acronym of an Islamic resistance movement identifying itself as a "Palestinian Sunni-Islamic fundamentalist militant and nationalist organization."

Ruled by the Palestinian Authority, the Palestinian territories are in the West Bank, or Israel's heartland of Judea and Samaria. Jews view Israel as the inheritance given them through covenant with the God of Israel established with Abraham, Isaac, Jacob, and their descendants.

Israel stretches 263 miles (424 km.) north to south and stretches from 71 miles (114 km.) to 9.3 miles (15 km.) wide at its narrowest point.

Southern Israel is dominated by the Negev Desert covering 6,178 sq. miles (16,000 km2), more than half of the nation's land area. The northern Negev contains the Judean Desert, which, at its border with Jordan, includes the Dead Sea (-417 meters or -1,368' below sea level), Earth's lowest point.

Central interior Israel includes the beautiful rolling Judean hills west of Jerusalem. Its central and northern coastline contains flat, fertile coastal plains. The northern region includes the Mount Carmel Mountain range stretching inland through the productive Jezreel Valley to the hills of Galilee. The Sea of Galilee lies beyond, bordered on the east by the Golan Heights and on the north by Mount Hermon, Israel's highest point at 7,336 feet or 2,236 meters. Called the "snowy mountain" and the "gray-haired mountain," it is considered "the eyes of the nation" because its elevation makes it Israel's strategic early warning system.

Understanding Israel's geography helps visitors choose and schedule wisely the things they wish to see and do. My visits have taken me throughout the land during all four seasons, and I've loved them all. Depending on calendar dates and climate choices, plan travels to match ideal conditions. For example, those arriving in winter may start in Eilat on the Red Sea where Israel's narrowest point borders Egypt and Jordan and journey north from there. In the process, travelers will see flocks of migrating birds doing the same as they fly from Africa to Europe each spring and back again each fall seeking ideal weather—birds like storks, cranes, bee-eaters, Israel's national bird, the hoopoe, and countless others.

Experts claim that during migration season, over five hundred million birds fly through Israel, calling their journey, "the eighth wonder of the world." It's amusing that several years ago an eagle was trapped by a hunter in the Maronite Catholic town of Ashqout, Lebanon who noticed the bird had a tag around its ankle. The tag bore the word Israel, an abbreviation for Tel Aviv University, plus the number 5278. It also carried a transmitter on its back. The man thought the eagle might be an Israeli Mossad spy on a secret mission so turned the eagle over to Lebanese security authorities.

Their thorough investigation proved the eagle innocent.

Months earlier, Egyptian authorities detained a stork that a citizen thought might be a spy because it also carried a transmitter on its back. However, that transmitter was manufactured in France and that bird was also judged innocent. Apparently, cases of mistaken bird nationality occur every so often.

Travelers preferring cooler climates might start their journeys in Israel's far north near its border with Lebanon where Mount Hermon reaches 6693 feet. Operating year-round with natural or artificial snow, its chairlift carries passengers to fabulous views on Mount Hermon's peak. Its ski and snowboard lodge in the Israeli Golan Heights is surrounded by beautiful Hermon Nature Reserve near Banias, an important biblical site.

Originally Banias, but now Caesarea-Philippi, Banias is where Roman citizens dedicated a spring arising from a natural cave to the Greek god, Pan, in New Testament times, and later added three more niche shrines there. That pagan setting is where the disciple Peter first acknowledged Jesus as the Christ. The town that grew up around Banias is now a major archaeological dig.

On my first trip to Israel, I was devastated when my camera's battery suddenly died while hiking there, and I missed what I thought would be a once-in-a-lifetime shot. The forest path paralleled a scenic stream rushing to a waterfall bordered by white, pink, and peach wild cyclamen. I was inconsolable. I am thankful that later opportunities did arise, I've been there often, and eventually got great photos.

## Israel's Primary Geographical Zones

- The Mediterranean Coastal Plain (think California, Spain, Italy, and Europe's Mediterranean Coast)
- The Central (Judean) Hills
- The Jordan River Valley, part of our planet's Great Rift
- The Negev Desert

Israel's western border is its 170 mile or 273 km. coastline along the Mediterranean Sea where visitors find stunning beaches and good fishing. A bronze whale statue in Jaffa/Joppa/Yafo near Tel Aviv, commemorates Jonah's story. Impressive breakers crash against shore all the way from Gibraltar and along Africa's coasts. At night, one hears their roar long before the waves reach shore.

Israel's eastern boundary is part of the Great Rift Valley stretching south into mid-Africa. It includes the Jordan River and Dead Sea areas where many important archaeological sites are timeless windows into the land's earliest events. The Dead Sea itself is a world-famous resource for extracting the minerals used in cosmetics and creams distributed worldwide.

Farther south, travelers may snorkel or scuba dive year-round in the Red Sea. Over one hundred types of coral and eight hundred varieties of fish and sea life flourish in abundance second only to Australia's Great Barrier Reef. Visitors may climb nearby Mount Sinai, tour St. Catherine's Monastery, and/or spend time on a Negev camel ranch to explore timeless hot burning sands from the backs of these swaying ships of the desert.

Israel's compass points, North, East, South and West, offer scenes the patriarchs saw when they entered the Promised Land to receive inheritance everywhere the soles of their feet trod. Those ancient sites, as well as the modern cities of Tel Aviv, Jerusalem, and Haifa, along with smaller towns, kibbutzes, and encampments, all guarantee that time spent in Israel brings history to life while also adding memorable modern-day experiences.

In Israel's northern interior, the Sea of Galilee, also called Gennesaret and Kinneret because of its "harp" or "lyre" shape, is another must-see area. This large freshwater lake is around 13 miles long and 7 miles wide, averages 150 feet deep, and is 650 feet below sea level. Inspired pilgrims come to see where Jesus lived and performed New Testament miracles such as healing, walking on water, calming the storm, feeding multitudes, and many more.

Forty-minute to one-hour boat tours are available at reasonable cost. The scenes and memories are worth it.

Other than accidentally experiencing tear gas once due to a shortcut that put Cindy and me in the wrong place at a tense time, my experiences throughout Israel over nearly four decades have brought wonderful experiences with no close calls (so far).

## Once You're in the Land and on Your Way

Since we spend significant time and money on trips, I consider them major events—not whirlwind tours. Travelers benefit by staying long enough to connect personally with places and people, not just breeze through a list of names and places that mean little more than taking photos or buying a handful of postcards in souvenir shops to remind you of where you've been. Create valuable memories.

Local botanical gardens are high on my list of things to see as well as museums and local places of historic interest. Many are low cost or even free.

Check area museums. Most offer senior or student discounts when showing proof of age or connections to places of higher education. Passports or most official ID cards are accepted. In Spain, the only proof I had of my university connection was my photocopier card, but that brought significant savings there as well as at England's Tower of London.

When asked, most locals are happy to share tips on their area's history and local travel. It is possible to hire a taxi and driver for an agreed amount of time or take day or half-day tours. Riding buses has given me great travel experiences as drivers often enjoy showing off their local areas. One driver near George Town on Grand Cayman Island stopped his bus along a coastal highway and urged his passengers to get off to photograph that beautiful coastline with its active spouting blow hole. I love seeing places through the eyes of its residents rather than through the filtered lens of highly organized but impersonal tours.

Senior Citizen Discounts, Student Rates, and off-Peak season rates are available in most countries. I love Spain's high-speed Renfe trains—and generous discounts. For a low cost, I bought a card at Madrid's Atocha station that made me a recognized Spanish senior citizen for a year. I saved more on one ticket than the card cost.

Many other nations follow suit. If travelers are in Israel long enough, it is worth buying discounted light rail and/or train passes. Israel Railway (Rakevet Yisrae'el) is the state-owned system providing inter-city, commuter, and freight service. Children up to age five and senior citizens receive discounts.

Professional discounts are also often extended within many career groups. Check to see if you qualify. Such inquiry might also let you meet and enjoy your career counterparts in Israel. Sometimes great relationships result.

**Prolonged Stays and Living Abroad**

Most nations offer various senior citizen discounts which make holidaying or even living there cheaper than you might imagine.

Once again, Spain is a great example of discounts for transportation, museums, food, and much more, providing good value for inexpensive holidays or long-term stays. Investigate these for the areas you wish to visit in Israel before your trip. They appreciate tourism so often add perks to make stays attractive. Some sites limit discounts to Israeli senior citizens or students only, but most extend them to all.

Some travelers' ideas of heaven may be major shopping

adventures or days of spa luxury. Others may wish to get up close and personal to nature through birding or wildlife observation. Or enjoy a week at the beach in total relaxation. Or join a working kibbutz or moshav helping harvest or tend animals or perhaps help with a sheep, goat, cattle, or camel drive and enjoy shared meals afterward.

Through research and inquiries, it's possible to find perfect travel opportunities for individuals or families. Take time to make ideal arrangements—it's worth it. Careful planning lets you design your days to fit each exact budget and bucket list. It's also often possible to locate flight, rail, and travel discounts or coupons for further options, as well as occasional fabulous Groupons. One allowed my older son and me to enjoy a hot air balloon ride we'll never forget at a fair price.

I had a year to plan my first trip to Israel so explored many avenues ahead of time. That trip lasted 36-days and covered Israel from the Mediterranean to the Jordan River and mountains plus orchards along Israel's border with Lebanon to its Sinai boundary with Egypt and the Red Sea besides strategic stops in Europe getting to Israel and back.

When my youngest grandson, Rocco, turned five, our extended family visited St. Paul, Minnesota's Science Museum, the most visited museum in the Midwest. Rocco raced ahead to see dinosaurs, robots, and science models, keeping us busy chasing him. But suddenly the small human whirlwind stopped and said, "Wait! Where's Grandma?" My family has often asked that question since. Sometimes I even wake up and ask myself where I am.

Besides making phone calls, sending emails, and communicating via Facebook, I send postcards while away to keep my family informed and entertained. My grandchildren love receiving picture cards and have started collections of their own that will probably interest them in travel.

When my five-year-old granddaughter received her most recent card, she said, "This deserves a frame." Her seven-year-old sister said her postcard of Irish castles now hangs on her wall. Both girls will receive more. I also buy postcards to remember places I can't personally visit.

Meanwhile various currencies, coins, foreign language newspapers, and many other inexpensive unique items I've brought home from everywhere have received considerable interest plus enhanced school projects for my grandchildren and their friends.

**Arrival Meeting Points**

In my personal travel, Denmark's Copenhagen (Kastrup) Airport wins top prize for giving the best and easiest-to-follow customer assistance to arriving passengers. I consider Amsterdam's Schiphol Airport to be a close second.

Jane, a lovely Danish university student, had lived in our home in Canada for a year. Now I got to visit her. Exotic distant names flashed on the destinations board showing me I was far from home: Ulan Bator, Moscow, Vladivostok, Pyongyang, Beijing, and Osaka. Surrounded by surging humanity, I craned my neck all directions, but didn't see Jane. It had been ten years. Would I recognize her? Would she recognize me?

I wasn't sure how to proceed and wished I had a back-up plan. These were pre-cell phone days. I knew French and smatterings of German but no Danish. How could I request help? Just then I spotted the first of six Meeting Point signs overhead marked with red arrows. An Assistance Center was also identified on a big yellow board labeled in several languages. Its welcoming desk staff arranges meet and greet, fast track, transit support, baggage help, and probably any service needed. They page the people travelers need to connect with and maintain a message board besides helping deaf, blind, or visually impaired passengers.

I had Jane's phone number but no way to call. A friendly man at the desk used his own phone to reach Jane. Traffic had delayed her and her husband. Yes, we recognized each other and had a wonderful time.

Any of those helpful courtesy steps would have helped reunite my scattered team on a later trip to Israel when eight of us landed in Tel Aviv on three different planes within thirty minutes of each other.

I love most things about Israel but hope Ben Gurion Airport improves its Meeting Point passenger assistance service unless my dilemma happened on an exceptionally demanding day. It is one of the world's largest airports, handling over twenty-five million passengers per year. Perhaps their meeting service system is fine when the right steps are followed. Sadly, we found my teammates and I had not communicated well enough to avoid terrifying chaos.

In 2016, a CNN article named Ben Gurion's security as the safest in the world, adding that many of their protocol steps are implemented in other parts of the world. Arriving passengers pass through Customs, recover their luggage, and are checked by a security officer. A yellow coding system 10-digit number is taped on the back of passports.

The number indicates the security risk level each passenger is believed to represent. The first number, from one to six, the highest possible being six, indicates the traveler's perceived threat level.

Those scoring high are taken aside for extra screening. Once approved, large stainless-steel doors open for individuals to leave the luggage area to enter the airport's immense lobby beyond. There, arrivals hopefully meet their teammates or the people there to collect them. If there are delays, arriving passengers may wait in seats by the far wall in front of a bookstore. There are also convenient restrooms and ATMs nearby and a food kiosk selling sandwiches and beverages.

The second popular meeting option there is in front of the bronze bust of Ben Gurion near Gate 2 that arriving passengers see as soon as they leave Security to enter the airport hall. There is no seating there, so those waiting must stand, but that isn't normally a problem. A second statue of Ben Gurion is located just outside the main airport doors, so if you make his statue your meeting point, be sure to check both locations. Large crowds of departing and arriving passengers constantly mill through the airport.

Be very clear with fellow travelers about where and when to meet. Flight arrival boards help and one large sign posted in the arrival hall says Meeting Point. However, no one was there when I first went there for help. The young woman who arrived later could not solve my dilemma.

Hopefully, all will go well for other travelers, and they will land on time without incident. Let me add, I have successfully rendezvoused with travel-team members in Paris for flights originating in Atlanta or Minneapolis to continue on to Israel. We also successfully rendezvoused in Amsterdam for flights originating in Halifax, Nova Scotia, Canada, and Minneapolis to fly on to Israel without problem. One traveler who flew with me from Minneapolis had come from Colorado to meet me so we could fly on together from there. Perhaps those trouble-free connections made me over-confident. May this example be helpful in the event you need to negotiate such connections.

Let me emphasize—be clear and precise in defining exact meeting points and times. It did not occur to me that any detail of our plan could go wrong. Also, it's smart to be sure each team member has everyone else's contact details, up-to-date flight information, full trip schedule and hotel or hostel reservation confirmations in advance in case teammates get separated, plus a means to phone or text one another.

Once when overtired, I left the printed pages containing my contact information at an airport check-in counter at departure and had to rely on memory. Thankfully, the friend who met me in Manila, Philippines at the other end of that trip arrived on time and found me. On another journey, I mistakenly left the printed itinerary in my checked bag instead of in my carry-on. Life is easier these days when so much information can be stored digitally in cell phones or any other apparatus. Because drained batteries, accidents, or theft can make even digital devices fail, I recommend carrying one printed paper copy with all itinerary information as well.

Teamwork matters, but failures also provide learning opportunities. The leader may not always possess all of the answers. Hopefully, each member contributes. On another trip to Israel, we had a day-long layover in Amsterdam, I had arranged in advance to rendezvous with dear married friends serving in the U.S. military in nearby Brussels. Shelly and Sean knew our arrival time, and we knew theirs, so we intently searched to find them in the crowded plaza near Amsterdam's Central Train Station. In that mass of humanity, faces blurred. My teammates didn't know my friends except for seeing my grainy photo. I began to think our rendezvous had failed when our newest team member said, "What about that couple over there? They look like they're searching for someone. Could that be them?"

It was. Everything came into focus and I hugged my friends' necks. They and I had both nearly given up hope of finding each other. We had a great time and I gained appreciation for the observation skills of our newest team member when mine had failed.

In 2018, I led seven friends to Israel for two weeks. It was the first visit there for five of them. Four of us flew together from Memphis to Tel Aviv, one from Atlanta, and three from Dallas. The one flying from Dallas got a better price when being routed through Germany. No problem, these were seasoned travelers. We agreed to pass through Customs, claim our luggage, and then meet in the large outer terminal area. To me that meant grabbing our suitcases, passing through Security quickly, and meeting in the large arrival hall after exiting Security and passing through the forbidding stainless-steel doors. It did not occur to me that travelers might linger in the luggage area.

Flights don't always arrive on time. Ours landed early, but the flight through Germany touched down late. Excited to gather my group, I rushed through Customs, grabbed my suitcase, breezed through Security, and exited the steel doors to scan the arrival hall crowd for my other seven people. Nada. I didn't recognize a soul and did not realize I was actually the first to leave Security. I had planned to rent an Israeli phone in the terminal after gathering my friends so didn't yet have a communication method in place.

Minutes later, the husband of the Dallas couple joined me looking distraught. One of their suitcases had been delayed. He left his wife in the luggage area and exited Security to find the baggage office and file a report. However, after passing through the now closed steel doors, he could not reenter. Even worse, his wife carried both passports. Without his, the Security officers could not allow him to re-enter to rejoin her.

On previous trips through this airport, I had not noticed a row of chairs along the far wall of the baggage area. Why put chairs in an area where no one lingers? Our team-member routed through Germany did not know I had already arrived. She thought it would be a good idea for her and the others to collect their luggage and sit in those chairs in the baggage area to wait until I appeared. Her idea might have worked if our planes all had been on schedule.

Those who knew I had arrived but gone ahead, figured I would come back for them. Even the Dallas wife did not realize that her husband could not pass through Security to return.

I had reserved two rental cars. We picked up one that day to use during our first two days in Jaffa-Tel Aviv where most things we would see and do were within walking distance of our hostel. It saved money to get the second car on the morning we would drive north. Therefore, I had prepaid a taxi to take four of our people and their luggage to our Tel Aviv hostel. (Now days we could have boarded the light rail train right outside the arrival hall to the left of the passenger exit, but I didn't know that then.)

Our taxi driver came to our agreed-upon meeting point, the statue of Ben Gurion at the arrival hall's back wall. I explained our delay and asked him to wait. He leaned against the statue and checked his watch. Our arrangement only required him to wait thirty minutes before leaving. Now, it had been over twenty, and the clock was ticking.

Desperate, I risked an expensive international call on my iPhone but couldn't reach any of our team. (Poor reception in a noisy airport.) I learned later my friends in baggage had also tried to phone me but couldn't get through either. Their voicemail reached me one hour later. The capable Dallas retired military husband asked officials to help. They said he needed to start over and enter Security at a distant point as if he were leaving Israel, but he couldn't do that without his passport. I had my passport but didn't want to repeat the entire Security process again either.

I approached the steel doors separating us from Security and waited until they opened for a passenger to exit. As one did, I glimpsed the Dallas gentleman's wife across the divide and signaled her as madly as any sea captain waves semaphores to avoid shipwreck. She gathered the others. By the time we eight reunited, we had flown over seventeen hours, felt stretched and grumpy— not an auspicious trip beginning. Our taxi driver did wait and appreciated the generous tip he earned.

That taught me to be super-clear and specific in instructions about where and when to meet and to have a back-up plan. Since then, I plan meticulously and/or delegate so someone has a usable phone/text system in place the minute we land. We gladly share expenses for nearly everything, including phone rental, SIM cards, etc.

During one trip, an unavoidable last-minute cancellation at one accommodation meant four of us had to stay two miles away from the other four during our eight days in Jerusalem. We attempted to do everything together so it would not affect our plans, but that wasn't easy.

Guiding even close friends in two cars is like herding cats.

Since then, I only take teams the size I can fit into one vehicle and make sure we share spacious accommodations or have adjoining suites.

On early trips to Israel, we walked or sometimes drove to Gethsemane and occasionally found parking. Today, it's better to bus, taxi, or walk to that popular destination. On our 2019 trip, we left our condo after lunch for the beautiful site at the foot of the Mount of Olives across the Brook Kidron from the Old City's Eastern or Golden Gate. MapQuest estimated the four-mile drive would take thirty minutes, which seemed long since it wasn't a holiday or rush hour, but we soon found ourselves in bumper-to-bumper traffic. We inched forward and soon realized we could have walked faster.

MapQuest's time estimate proved to be too conservative. It took over an hour to travel the four miles. As expected, parking was available only for big tour buses, so I dropped my passengers at the site entrance. Since I had enjoyed Gethsemane before, I was willing to miss seeing it this time if I could not find parking. My plan was to drive up the narrow road to the top of the Mount of Olives, the site of Jesus's ascension, and then turn around and descend to pick up my passengers by the time they finished enjoying the garden and church.

Even managing the drive to the top of the Mount and back in thirty minutes proved impossible. Traffic uphill couldn't progress because large vans coming down from the top honked and hurtled past. One brushed so near, it bumped my car mirror flat against our vehicle. I restored its position. Windows down on a hot day, the next van driver used his hand to push my mirror flat again as he squeaked by. I expected to hear the grinding sound of metal on metal and am still amazed I didn't. I'm still amazed that the van driver didn't scrape off paint as he squeaked by.

I soon gave up hope of ascending and instead tried nosing forward in tiny increments to reverse and turn around without reaching the top, but more descending vehicles whizzing by made that impossible. A kindly Arab grandfather signaled me directions but intimidating massive stone walls were so near, I couldn't succeed.

Two Arab youths approached. One offered to lift his hand to stop traffic while the other jockeyed my car around. They looked trustworthy. I was desperate and grateful. They succeeded in less than a minute and wouldn't take money but got my biggest smile.

My left foot had pressed the brake so long and hard, my leg could barely hold me when I climbed out. By then my passengers had finished seeing Gethsemane and the church and come to the road to find me. They witnessed the last part of my ordeal and worried about my safety and sanity—with just cause. They hopped in and we rolled away, but I vowed never to drive to Gethsemane again. I'm happy my friends enjoyed their experience but negotiating that short distance for an intense and prolonged time has been my worst driving saga in Israel to date.

However you reach Gethsemane, seeing its wonderful garden is a must. Its ancient olive trees are far more protected now than during my 1984 first visit. Today a fenced walkway surrounds the perimeter so visitors may see but not approach the several thousand-year-old trees and walk among them as tourists were privileged to do in previous times.

It's easy to imagine Jesus and his disciples kneeling there under the gray-green leaf canopies. He went "a stone's throw further" to travail for the trial awaiting him while his three closest disciples yielded to sleep, overcome by sorrow. Thick-barked, gnarled trunks too wide to stretch my arms around made me want to kneel, too. These same trees had been there then.

Today there is no accessible space in the garden to kneel. There is space for reflection in the beautiful adjacent Church of All Nations, a Roman Catholic basilica open to people of all faiths. Also known as the Church of the Agony, the front altar area is built around the rock on which Jesus is believed to have prayed in anguish. This church is another location where history and faith seamlessly intersect.

Those visitors wishing to negotiate another narrow twisting roadway slightly south and a bit up the Mount, will find the exquisite Church of the Teardrop representing Jesus's prayer as he wept over Jerusalem as told in Matthew, chapter 23, "Jerusalem, Jerusalem, how often would I have gathered thy children together, even as a hen gathereth her chickens under her wings, and ye would not."

The view inside and out is stupendous, again mingling faith and history. Its official name is Dominus Flevit, in Latin meaning "The Lord Wept." It is built in the shape of a tear drop to commemorate the Lord's tears over Jerusalem.

On one trip as friends and I enjoyed seeing both the Garden of Gethsemane and this church, a pleasant Arab guide attached himself to us and led us to a nearby gift shop with good prices run by his friends, and then to a restaurant at the top of the Mount run by his relatives who served amazing food at fair cost. He phoned a cousin who brought a camel and gave short rides for $5 each. Then the guide offered to whisk us into Jordan for a fun day-long trip without visas, saying he did it all the time, usually for international airline pilots.

We balked. Several years previously, two American hikers had accidentally wandered across a border into the Islamic Republic of Iran and began serving a three-year sentence until US diplomacy extricated them. We enjoyed the cheerful guide, but warning bells rang against us illegally entering any foreign country.

If an opportunity sounds too good to be true, it usually is. If it involves breaking the law, don't! If there is a place you truly want to see, spend the time and effort to make proper legal arrangements and enjoy the experience without hazard.

**Tel Aviv Free Walking Tours**—a great way to the see the city is on foot. Enjoy free English-language guided tours of Tel Aviv's top sights plus go-it-alone tours. These guided tours do not require advance booking; just show up at the designated meeting point.

**The Old Jaffa Tour** every Wednesday at 9:30 a.m. winds through the Flea Market, the Old City, past older archeological sites, and up to Hapisga Garden. The landmark clock tower is the meeting point. Other free tours are available through the day and many have English-speaking guides. Voluntary donations are appreciated for these truly excellent tours.

**The Tel Aviv University Tour** is available every Monday at 11 a.m. (except for Jewish holidays). This tour introduces Israeli architecture on campus explaining their styles, international influences, stories of buildings and architects, plus showing environmental sculpture and landscape design. The tour is given in cooperation with the Friends of Tel Aviv University. The meeting point is the Dyonon bookstore, campus entrance (the intersection of Haim Levanon and Einstein streets). Tourists can pick up DIY selfguided maps at the municipality's Visitor Center.

**Rabin Square** is the main plaza outside City Hall named for Israeli Prime Minister Yitzhak Rabin who was assassinated there on November 4, 1995, at the end of a peace rally.

**Ben-Gurion House** is a small but good museum and is often overlooked. Located at 17 Ben-Gurion Boulevard, this house served as an additional residence for Israel's first Prime Minister, David Ben-Gurion. Visitors can see his library, family living area, and the study where he worked. This free guided tour reveals much about Ben-Gurion's life and work.

**The Nahalat Binyamin Craft Fair**, next to the Carmel Market in one of Tel Aviv's oldest districts, is a wonderful event on Tuesdays and Fridays. It features over two hundred artists gathering to display and sell their works.

**Tel Aviv University's Botanical Gardens.** These magnificent gardens, covering 34,000 square meters, display many of the world's best species of flora and fauna. Located in the heart of Tel Aviv University, visitors may also tour the plant museum Sundays through Thursdays, from 8 a.m. to 4 p.m. Phone ahead (972-3-6409910) as the garden is also an outdoor classroom for the university students.

**Jerusalem City Walking Tours**—Every Saturday all year, the Jerusalem municipality hosts free guided walking tours. Licensed English-speaking guides show different neighborhoods along interesting streets past historical structures through the city. Travelers should decide which route interests them most before selecting a three-hour informative walk.

**Bezalel Street Fair**—like the Nahalat Binyamin craft fair in Tel Aviv, the Bezalel arts and crafts street fair offers creativity every Friday between 10 a.m. and 4 p.m. The fair began as a weekly gathering for families, tourists, and artists. Stroll past craft stalls to glimpse the best of Israel's creative communities. The market is between Bezalel Street and Shmuel HaNagid Street next to the old home of the Bezalel Academy of Arts and Design, Israel's national art school.

**Yad Hashmona**, west of Jerusalem in the Judean hills, is a unique community founded by Finnish Christians in memory of eight (hashmona) Austrian Jewish refugees who escaped to Finland but were surrendered to the Nazis. Finnish-heritage and Israeli followers of Jesus (Yeshua) live there today in a collective moshav offering good tourist accommodations, a restaurant, and a free beautiful biblical garden overlooking the Judean hills.

Planning ahead is key to increasing enjoyment as travelers choose the places and activities they want to see in each location. Before traveling, hometown public libraries offer great materials on most countries. These days, wonderful additional resources are available online, on TV programs, YouTube, and on travel sites created and maintained by fellow travelers. During or following trips, friends and the public appreciate seeing your photos and reports posted on social media if you're willing.

During trips, I keep a personal travel journal. On my first journeys to new destinations, my journal is lengthy. After two weeks in the Philippines in 2008, my journal held 11,250 words. That report was partly a gift to an American missionary family who had invested years of service there until their ages and health did not permit them to continue.

If I have visited an area previously, I just update my notes with new names, places, and experiences. Journals are wonderful memory-keepers to read and read again. My detailed information is also requested so surprisingly often, it led to me writing this book.

**Major Destinations Alphabetically**

Israel's four holiest cities are Hebron, Jerusalem, Safed, and Tiberias. Here is an alphabetical listing of Israel's most-visited cities and towns.

**Acre/Akko** has been shaped through time by the Romans, Ottomans, Crusaders, Mamelukes, Byzantines, and British. It currently has a mixed population of Jews, Christians, and Muslims. Old City Akko is a UNESCO World Heritage City.

**Afula**, a city in Israel's Northern district, is called the "Capital of the Valley" for its strategic location in the Jezreel Valley. It is known as Ofel in the Bible, the hometown of Gideon in Judges, chapters 6–8. Elisha, the disciple to Elijah, lived in the area.

**Arad** is a city in Israel's Southern District on the border between the Negev and Judean Deserts west of the Dead Sea and east of Beersheba. Judges, chapter 1 describes it as a Canaanite stronghold whose king refused to let the Israelites cross from the desert to the Judean Mountains. Tel Arad is a surprisingly interesting active archaeology dig site worth seeing. On one trip, we loved and enjoyed our accommodation there at Villa 1000 at 43 Bareket Street, Arad 89067 Israel. It is managed by a wonderful, knowledgeable owner/hostess who provides amazing breakfasts!

**Ashdod**, Israel's sixth-largest city and major port, is north of Ashkelon but south of Tel Aviv on the Mediterranean Coast. After Joshua conquered the Promised Land, Ashdod was given to the tribe of Judah in Joshua 15. It is named as one of the principal Philistine cities in I Samuel 6 along with Gath, Gaza, Ekron, and Ashkelon. After the Philistines captured Israel's Ark of the Covenant, they placed it in the temple of Dagon in Ashdod.

**Ashkelon/Ashqelon/**or **Ascalon** is a coastal city in Israel's Southern District along the Mediterranean Coast south of Tel Aviv. Twelve miles north of Gaza, ancient Tel Ashkelon was a powerful city built and rebuilt under Canaanites, Philistines, and Romans. In Judges, chapters 14-16, it is where Delilah cut Samson's hair. A project is underway to present the archaeological remains of this site in a manner fitting its former glory. Goals are to restore the site's Roman basilica and Odeon.

**Atlit** is a coastal town south of Haifa founded in 1903 as a Jewish village under Baron Edmond de Rothschild's sponsorship. The British established a detention center nearby to intern those eager to enter Israel during its British Mandate before legal immigration was possible. Today the Atlit camp is a museum and National Heritage Site. The ruins of a submerged Neolithic village lie off the coast. A Crusader outpost there fell in 1291 AD/CE.

**Beth Shan/Beit She'an** in Israel's Northern District, also known historically as Scythopolis, has played an important role due to its location where the Jordan River and Jezreel Valleys join. In I Samuel 31, the Bible describes the Israelites fighting the Philistines on nearby Mount Gilboa, resulting in the bodies of King Saul and three of his sons being hung on the city's walls until rescued for burial by the men of Jabesh-Gilead. In Roman times, Beth Shan/Beit She'an was a pleasure city and the leading city of the Decapolis.

**Beersheba/Be'er Sheva**, meaning *"Well of the Oath"* is the largest population center in southern Israel's Negev Desert, and Israel's fourth largest overall. The oath between Abraham and Abimelech is reported in Genesis and Abraham's well is there, important to three religions. Tel Be'er Sheva National Park, identified as biblical Beersheba, is the large local archaeological site very worth visiting. Lakiya, a nearby modern Bedouin village, offers beautiful "Embroideries of the Desert" items for sale.

**Beit Shemesh** was named by the Canaanites after Shapash/Shemesh, their sun-goddess. Ruins of that ancient Canaanite/Israelite city are visible at Tel Beit Shemesh. In Joshua 15, the Bible names the city as belonging to the tribe of Judah near its border with the tribe of Dan.

**Bethlehem** in the central West Bank is six miles south of Jerusalem. Its name means "House of Bread." David the shepherd boy was born and crowned king there. Rachel's tomb is an important Jewish holy site at the city's northern entrance. Christian pilgrims visit the Church of the Nativity to see the believed birthplace of Jesus and the nearby Shepherds' Field. However, due to conflict, the Arab Christian population has declined in recent years.

**Kanna/Cana**, the town five miles northeast of Nazareth in Galilee, northern Israel, is the site of the wedding feast where Jesus performed his first miracle by turning water into wine.

**Dimona** is an Israeli city in the Negev Desert southeast of Beersheba and west of the Dead Sea. The nation's only nuclear reactor and research facility are nearby. A bus I once rode to Eilat took a break near Dimona. I crossed the road to photograph an open view with distant palm trees. Apparently, the reactor complex was somewhere in that direction because across the road, two men rose from nowhere and told me to stop taking pictures or they would confiscate my camera. I complied.

**Eilat/Elath** at Israel's extreme southern tip, is the nation's Red Sea port resort town famous for beautiful beaches and clear sparkling waters great for snorkeling and diving. It borders Taba, Egypt to the south, Jordan's Red Sea port of Aqaba to the east, Haql, Saudi Arabia, is visible to the southeast across the Gulf, and it is the departure point to reach Mount Sinai (Jabal Musa). A nature reserve offers underwater trails among fish-filled reefs and an underwater marine park observatory offers a glass-enclosed observation center. I tried snorkeling the one time I visited Hawaii but am not good at it.

When my son, Aaron, joined me in Israel, I loved watching him scuba dive in the Red Sea. I was amazed that whether on shore or swimming, I could also see plentiful colorful marine life in the magically warm water. Aaron did a double-take when he noticed nudist sunbathers on the beach.

"Mom, is that a flesh-colored bathing suit, or...?"

"Yes—a birthday suit."

That woman was generously proportioned. Aaron turned brighter red than his sunburn.

For Cindy and my first visit to Eilat, Tina recommended that we stay at The Shelter, a pleasant inexpensive Christian hostel mentioned in this book's "Remembrances of Israel" section. Their website reads, "We have had over 90,000 guests in The Shelter in our over thirty years of operation. Our guests have come from more than eighty-five countries." That is certainly true.

We had barely left the bus to begin looking for the place, dragging suitcases, when a polite young man approached us.

"You're going to The Shelter. Follow me. I will take you there."

Cindy and I looked at each other. How did he know? We had followed Tina's guidelines to dress like middle class Israeli women, not tourists—unless our well-made North American shoes gave us away. Whatever the clue, we followed him several blocks and he ushered us into the shady tree-dotted garden surrounding the hostel. By the time we registered, he had disappeared. Whoever he was, human or divine, we were grateful.

Unexpected help happens so frequently on trips in Israel, I've come to expect and always appreciate it. Inside the Shelter, we found guests of all ages, nationalities, and stimulating discussions.

That afternoon, Cindy and I set out to explore the beautiful desert oasis town. The Red Sea is so warm and clear, visitors easily spot tropical fish in all shapes, sizes, and colors whether they stand near at the water's edge or snorkel. If you don't wish to enter the water, visit the excellent aquariums. The border with Egypt is so close, we walked to the Taba/Menachem Begin Crossing but did not cross the border.

In local shops, we bought copper items from King Solomon's rediscovered mines that American Jewish rabbi and archaeologist Nelson Glueck found by looking where the Bible said they would be. His fascinating books describing his many discoveries are exciting reading.

As the sun passed its zenith, we explored attractive residential areas. One large estate had its wide metal latticework gates open, so it looked accessible to the public. A broad driveway swept past buildings to a beach with roped off swimming areas. We had bathing suits under our clothes so swam in the nearest section. We noticed posted signs we couldn't read with our glasses off, but after our cooling swim, put our glasses on and read, "No swimming beyond this point—Shark-infested waters!"

That got our attention. We turned to leave but now the wrought iron gates were locked. I placed my feet between its lattice-work grill ladder rungs and easily climbed over the top to the sidewalk beyond and sat innocently on the bus stop bench right outside.

When Cindy started to climb, a woman rushed out of a building shouting and waving her arms as if they were weapons ready to shoot.

"Stop! What were you doing in here? How did get in? This is private property."

The lady didn't notice me—only poor blushing, stammering Cindy standing immediately in front of her, although she explained that the gates had been open and she had visited what she believed was a public beach.

"How could you not know?' The lady shrilled but gradually calmed. After shaking an admonishing finger at Cindy again, she unlocked the gate and ushered Cindy out just in time to board the city bus that rolled up to whisk us away. We suffered no ill effects but acquired another lasting memory.

**Timna** (Timnah) Park is the interesting copper mining district 17 miles (or 27 km.) north of Eilat. An exact replica of the Tabernacle of Moses is also located there and open to the public.

**Ziklag** (Khirbet a-Ra'i) is a site in southern Israel where researchers believe they have found Ziklag. The town is noted in the Books of Joshua and Samuel as a Philistine town near Gath (for which Kiryat Gat is named). Radiocarbon dating ties the settlement to the early 10th century BC/BCE, the period associated with the life of King David.

**The Galilee** region in Israel's Northern District is divided into Lower and Upper portions. Both border the Sea of Galilee, but the Upper portion is more mountainous. The area is famous as the childhood home of Jesus and includes many major scenes associated with his ministry and miracles.

**Gaza/Gaza City**, is the largest center in the Gaza Strip. Inhabited since the 15th century BC/BCE, it has been dominated by many peoples and empires. After freedom from Egyptian control, it became part of a five-city Philistine pentapolis. Its port flourished under Roman rule. After 635 AD/CE, Gaza was conquered by Muslims and became a center of Islamic law. The Crusaders occupied Gaza in 1099 AD/CE. During World War I, it fell to British forces and became part of Mandatory Palestine (Israel).

Captured by Israel in the 1967 Six-Day War, the West Bank (Judea and Samaria) returned to Israel's hands with part transferred to delegated control by the local Palestinian National Authority.

Today, that Authority has jurisdiction over Areas A and B while Israel solely administrates Area C. Fatah and Hamas political groups struggle between themselves regarding methods and goals for governing the parts under the Palestinian Authority.

The local economy is based on agriculture and small-scale industry. The population is Muslim with a Christian minority. In Bible times, Samson, the last of the Judges, spent a night there with Delilah. When his enemies laid in wait at the city gate, Samson tore it from its hinges and carried it thirty miles to the hill facing Hebron!

**Haifa** is built on the slopes of Mount Carmel facing the Mediterranean. Many compare its setting to San Francisco. With a history extending back three millennia, it has been conquered and occupied by Canaanites, Israelites, Phoenicians, Persians, Hasmoneans, Romans, Byzantines, Arabs, Crusaders, Ottomans, and the British. It is Israel's biggest, most industrialized port and the third largest city in rank after Jerusalem and Tel Aviv. Like Acre/ Akko, its multi-ethnic population is a success story modeling peaceful co-existence between Jews, Christians, and Muslims. Haifa is also the world center for the Baha'i Faith and its famous gardens. In Bible times, the prophet Elijah lived in a cave on Mount Carmel and prayed for rain to end the three-year drought during Ahab's reign. Elijah later confronted and destroyed the prophets of Baal.

**Hebron** is a largely Arab city south of Jerusalem, the West Bank's biggest population center and the second largest in the Palestinian territories. The area is important to Jews, Christians, and Muslims as the traditional burial site of Abraham and Sarah, Isaac and Rebekah, and Jacob and Leah in the Cave of the Patriarchs. Jews consider it the second holiest city after Jerusalem.

There is a small enclave of Jews settled in Hebron where there has always been a Jewish presence.

**Jaffa/Joppa/Yafo** is one of the oldest port cities in Israel and the Mediterranean. Due to its natural and strategic advantages with a hill above a bay, the city has been the site of historical events over thousands of years, its ancient port being in use since Phoenician times. It is the destination II Chronicles identifies for where King Hiram of Tyre floated the cedar logs King Solomon needed carried to Jerusalem for building his temple and palace. Many other Bible stories, like Jonah, the Apostle Peter staying at Simon the Tanner's House, the raising of Dorcas/Tabitha, and others are tied to this area. Still a busy port, it is a more secular city than Jerusalem, it is also a major tourist destination and hosts an accomplished art colony.

**Jenin** is an Arab town in the northern West Bank under the jurisdiction of the Palestinian Authority that serves as an administrative center for surrounding towns.

**Jericho** is a large Arab city in the West Bank east of Jerusalem and west of the Jordan River under Israeli administration but governed by the Palestinian National Authority. Local springs have sustained human settlement there for thousands of years. The Bible describes it as the "city of palm trees." Considered one of the oldest continuously occupied cities on earth and with the oldest city wall, it is, of course, where "Joshua fought the battle of Jericho."

**Jerusalem** is Israel's largest and most populated city. Averaging 3,000-foot elevation and above, it is Israel's most defensible metropolis. Formerly Jebus, King David and his men captured it to make it his kingdom's capital. Its approximately one-kilometer square walled Old City is venerated by Jews, Christians, and Muslims. Divided into Muslim, Jewish, Armenian, and Christian Quarters, the city contains sites sacred to all three religions. The landmark Via Dolorosa route that Jesus walked carrying his cross on the way to crucifixion is especially meaningful to Christians. One interesting stop along that way marked by the Stations of the Cross is Lithostrotos, actually part of the ancient roadbed and courtyard where soldiers played a gambling game for Jesus' seamless robe.

Those marks, scratched in the stones, are still visible today.

**Old City Jerusalem's Gates**

Biblical scholars name twelve gates as far back as the Restoration period when Ezra and Nehemiah returned from Babylonian exile to rebuild Jerusalem. The Old City's original gates were rebuilt by Turkish Sultan Suleiman I, the Magnificent, in the early sixteenth century AD/CE. These are the eight gates best known today—the other four are less clearly identified.

**Zion Gate** on the south side of the wall, leads to the Jewish Quarter and Mount Zion. Bullet holes on the gate's façade are from battles that took place during the 1948 War of Independence. A short walk from Zion Gate leads to the Upper Room, site of the Last Supper, King David's Tomb, and a Dormition Abbey. Walking downhill for five to ten minutes along the southern walls of the Old City brings travelers to the Jewish Quarter and the Western Wall.

There is little public parking, but one area on Mount Zion next to

Zion Gate provides the nearest access to the Jewish Quarter and the Western Wall.

**The Dung Gate** (or Moghrabi or Silwan Gate) was built in the 16th century AD/CE. It is situated near the southeast corner of the Old City, southwest of the Temple Mount. Directly behind it is the entrance to the Western Wall Plaza.

**The Golden Gate** (or Eastern Gate or the Gate of Mercy) faces the Mount of Olives and may have been built as early as 520 AD/CE by the last Byzantine or first Arab rulers. One archaeologist believes that a still earlier gate lies beneath. This entrance gave pilgrims the most direct access to the Jewish Temple so Jews could approach as close as possible after the Temple was destroyed. It is probably the route Jesus traveled on Palm Sunday riding on a donkey. Sultan Suleiman had the double entrance gate sealed shut in 1541 AD/CE because scripture prophesies that on his return, Jesus will use that gate to re-enter Jerusalem.

**Lions' Gate** is also called St. Stephen's Gate, after the first Christian martyr who tradition says was stoned nearby. Lions' Gate is near the Pool of Bethesda and the Via Dolorosa.

**Herod's Gate**, near the Damascus Gate, is said to have no connection to the Judean king of that name. It grants access to the Old City's Muslim Quarter and to the large Israeli Arab and Palestinian neighborhoods beyond.

I led friends on one trip to Israel in the fall of 2014 during Sukkot, the Feast of Booths. Traffic in Jerusalem anytime can defy description but intensifies during major Jewish feast days. As we walked on foot, we saw two cars going opposite directions having a standoff as to which of them would pass through narrow Herod's Gate. One was driven by a woman trying to enter the Old City, the other by a rabbi ready to leave. Neither budged. Their dilemma required discussions with a policeman, the rabbi's young son, and a growing crowd on foot, on bikes, plus a young mother pushing a baby buggy, all giving advice and measurements on how near the rock walls both cars were and in danger of scraping (a real risk). We took photos, glad not to be involved. In comparison, North American traffic seemed unchallenging. We wondered who would win. After lengthy, loud discussions with much arm waving, the housewife surrendered and backed up her car. The rabbi went his way. I would like to have understood their conversation.

**The New Gate** was not part of Sultan Suleiman's sixteenth-century AD/CE wall rebuild.

**The Dung Gate** connects the Old City to the Valley of Hinnom where Judas hung himself after betraying Jesus. Nearby are the authentic first century AD/CE southern steps to the temple, still accessible and unchanged from the days that Jesus and His disciples used them. My friends and I agree a special atmosphere is still sensed by those privileged to climb the steps today.

**Gates Named for Their Destinations: Damascus Gate**—from this gate, the road leads north to Nablus (biblical Shechem or Sichem) and then on to Damascus, the capital of Syria.

**Jaffa Gate**—this was the destination for Jewish and Christian pilgrims who docked in Joppa/Jaffa/Yafo and made their way up to Jerusalem. As Jaffa Road enters Jerusalem, it bisects the city and is its biggest, best-known thoroughfare.

**Masada,** described earlier in the Where to travel in Israel section under Historic Sites, is King Herod's famous Dead Sea mountaintop fortress where nine hundred and sixty Jewish zealots chose death in 66 AD/CE rather than being captured by the Roman forces relentlessly besieging them.

**Metullah** is Israel's northernmost town on the Lebanese-Israeli border is a crossing into southern Lebanon and relies on agriculture and tourism from three beautiful nearby nature reserves.

**Nāblus,** also Nābulus, is a large Palestinian city in the upper West Bank formerly known as Shekhem/Shechem. This ancient city is the site of much Palestinian activism and is under the jurisdiction of the Palestinian Authority.

**Nazareth,** the largest city in Israel's Northern District is known as "the Arab capital of Israel." The inhabitants are largely Arab Israelis with around 70% Muslim and 30% Christian distribution. As the childhood home of Jesus, it is a center of Christian pilgrimage.

Its biblical history includes belief that the Basilica of the Annunciation is the site where the angel Gabriel told Mary she would bear a child. Nearby St. Joseph's Church is said to be the location of Joseph's carpentry workshop. An underground Synagogue Church is offered as the site where Jesus studied and prayed. Nazareth Village, a large open-air museum, re-enacts daily life in the time of Jesus.

**Nazareth Illit,** "Upper Nazareth," is a separate city with a Jewish population over 40,000.

**Ramla** is the only city founded in the Palestinian territories by Arabs. It was built from the ruins of nearby Lod (Lydda) and features the remains of a notable White Mosque and a Great Mosque. Traditionally the birthplace of Joseph of Arimathea, Franciscans gained permission to build a church and their friars assisted pilgrims. However, Napoleon's brief stay there caused the convent to be destroyed in retaliation by Muslims and the friars were killed.

**Ramallah** is an Arab city in the central West Bank thirteen miles north of Jerusalem that serves as the *de facto* administrative capital of the Palestinian National Authority (PNA). Historically, Ramallah was an Arab Christian town, but Muslims are now the majority population.

**Safed** in Israel's Northern District is the city with the highest elevation in Galilee and Israel. Fortified by Crusaders in the 1200s AD/CE. Since the sixteenth-century, Safed has been considered one of Judaism's Four Holy Cities, along with Jerusalem, Hebron, and Tiberias. It is the center of Kabbalah and Jewish mysticism.

**Sderot** is a western Negev development city in Israel's Southern District less than one mile east of Gaza. Its Jewish population has been a major target of Palestinian rocket attacks from the Gaza Strip, but Israel's Iron Dome defense system provides its residents good protection.

**Tel Aviv** meaning "Hill of Spring" is the new city built just north of ancient Jaffa/Joppa/Yafo. It was settled in 1909 on land that had previously been sand dunes and orange groves. Its planners laid out this first all-Jewish city in two thousand years with tall well-built apartment buildings along pleasant, broad, tree-lined boulevards reminiscent of European cities.

**Tiberias** is the largest city in Lower Galilee built by Herod Antipas in 18 AD/CE near natural hot springs and named for Roman Emperor Tiberias. As a Roman pleasure city, Beth Shan/Beit She'an has little connection to the life of Jesus. It was significant in Jewish history for being where the Jerusalem Talmud was composed and as the home of the Masoretes, Jewish scribe-scholars, who worked between the 6th and 10th centuries AD/CE primarily in Tiberias, Jerusalem, and Iraq. Its holy city status is due to many rabbis making the town a center for Jewish learning in the 18th and 19th centuries AD/CE.

There are seven cities under the jurisdiction of the Palestinian Authority that Israeli Jews cannot enter except by special permission, and usually with an IDF escort. They are Bethlehem, Jenin, Jericho, Nablus, Qalqilya, Ramallah, and Tulkarem.

**National Commemoration Events**

Each year, Israel's anniversary is celebrated in many locations. However, the observance is based on the specific Hebrew calendar date, so some years the event is observed in April and other times in May in our Julian calendar.

**Things to Do**

- Do decide and plan which destinations and experiences are most important to include on your trip.
- Do check on individual versus group admission rates if you're leading a team. Request senior and/or professional discounts where these apply as they're often available and granted.
- Do know something about each location's biblical, historical, and modern record before arriving so you don't miss important details. We had eaten lunch and bought gas in Afula several times, a city of 50,000 in the Jezreel

Valley, before I associated it with Ofel, the home of Gideon and connected to the prophet Elisha as well. I love learning and absorbing ALL I can of what has happened in each place.

- Do bargain in markets in the spirit of fun. If you are buying souvenirs or keepsakes, bargaining is an expected and often enjoyable art form in Israel and other countries. Several times when I've declined an offer, the shopkeeper has pursued me as I walked away brought along the item and a bag to finalize the sale. However, most often we agree on a price in the shop with both the seller and the buyer wearing smiles.

**Things Not To Do**

- Do not count on professional tours or guides showing you all major sites and events. To keep mileage costs and schedule times down, I'm shocked that many tours skip and don't even mention some very major destinations. I've talked to friends who've come to Israel on expensive tours but missed some very key sites. When I investigate, I see that tour routes have been shortened in ways that simplify the actual miles driven and the time involved.
- Do not haggle (unpleasantly dispute or bargain), over the cost of items for sale. Especially do not insult the shop, proprietor, or the merchandise—that is not good conduct anywhere and is not bargaining in the spirit of fun.

# 5
# DON'T MISS OUT

## Major Religious Events

Most visitors arrive in Israel with a list of some things they want to see and do. As time and schedules permit, here are my recommended places, events, and festivals to include if possible:

**Mount Carmel**—(near Haifa) is called a "holy mountain" in Egyptian records of the 16th century BC/BCE. It is where Elijah confronted the prophets of Baal in I Kings 18. Elijah's Prophet Cave can be reached by road or cable car. Greek inscriptions from Byzantine times are found on cave walls along with two drawings of a seven-branched menorah. This site is managed by Israel's Ministry of Religious Affairs at https://www.kkl-jnf.org/tourism-and-recreation/tours/elijah-mount-carmel-prophet.aspx

**Galilee**—Enjoy visiting as many sites associated with Jesus's ministry as time allows—Capernaum, Tabgha, the Mount of Beatitudes, St. Peter's Primacy, and more. Magdals is a wonderful newly-developed site at Migdal Junction near Tiberias. This *Smithsonian Magazine* article with photos describes it well— https://www.smithsonianmag.com/history/unearthing-world-jesus-180957515/

**Jerusalem**—The entire city, old and new, is fascinating. Be sure to see the Government Knesset buildings and the nearby Shrine of the Book next to the excellent Israeli Museum housing the Dead Sea Scrolls. Although the scrolls are no longer kept in the Rockefeller Museum, important work does continue there on the many fragments found alongside the famous Dead Sea manuscripts. In addition, a massive collection of other artifacts unearthed in the 1920s and 1930s is on free display in the Rockefeller Museum Sunday through Thursday from 10 a.m.–3 p.m. and from 10 a.m.– 2 p.m. on Saturdays. Parking is available on Saturdays.

**Ramat Rachel**—this kibbutz within Jerusalem's boundaries overlooks Bethlehem and contains Rachel's tomb, the burial place of the matriarch considered holy to Jews, Christians, and Muslims. Ramat Rachel offers nice accommodations and delicious food at good prices.

**Bethlehem**—visit the Church of the Nativity and nearby Shepherds' Field when conditions are calm. I've been once but don't stop during occasional times of unrest. Bethlehem is administered under the jurisdiction of the Palestinian Authority. Much of the Christian Arab population has left the area.

**Yardenit** is a beautiful baptismal site where the Jordan River leaves the Sea of Galilee. It represents the actual location further south where John the Baptist baptized Jesus.

**Yahud-Qasr al** is believed to be the actual site on the Jordan River north of the Dead Sea where John the Baptist baptized Jesus. It is also considered to be the place where the Israelites crossed the Jordan and where Elijah ascended to heaven. It had been unsafe until recent years when most active minefields have been cleared and those uncleared are well-marked with warning signs.

**The Dead Sea**–Take note of the salt crystals and remarkable scenery of this world-famous body of water -1,368 ft. (-417 meters) below sea level, the lowest point on Earth. Experience floating in the weightlessness, but don't get the salt water in your eyes.

**Ein Gedi**–the trail to the beautiful falls and pools important in the life of David as he fled from King Saul are within this National

Park. Visiting the restaurant and gift shop across the road marked Ein Gedi only is NOT enough. Also enjoy the flocks of antelopeappearing Nubian mountain goats and rock coneys or hyraxes inhabiting the area.

**Lakiya** or other Bedouin towns or encampments—In 1994, when visiting my American second cousin who lives in an Arab town near Beersheba, my son Aaron and I were privileged to attend a Bedouin wedding. My cousin introduced me to a covey of robed veiled women that I initially had difficulty distinguishing. We women sat outside under a canopy of trees. My cousin's father-inlaw had slaughtered two sheep and did much of the cooking to honor us and twenty other guests. Delicious food was served in round deep platters two feet across. We sat cross-legged in a circle and were given spoons. The men were not. Aaron was kept with the men in a different location because one gentleman smiled and said, "We keep men and women separate because we have learned not to mix gasoline with fire."

The first course was bulgur (soaked cracked wheat with dough wrapped around it), and big slabs of roast sheep with tasty whole spices on top. My cousin followed the custom of having me sit on her left and serving me choice pieces of meat that she pulled from the bones to pass my way. It was soon time to escort the bride from her house to the bridegroom's home.

The women of the village gathered to see her off. I did not know it at the time, but she was thirty years old and beautiful, a trained elementary teacher marrying her school's principal who was age forty-five. She would be his second wife but live in a separate home from his first wife and family who also attended. He had been urged not to take a second wife as an example to end the practice that to some degree continues there. I was told that adequate social services are not in place for unattached females so the practice of having multiple wives is seen as a way of looking after them.

In Bedouin manner, this young woman had not lived away from her family home before. Since these are typically arranged marriages, this initially appeared to be a somewhat fearful, sad occasion with tears flowing from the bride, family, and friends. However, traditional singing accompanied by drums gradually transitioned to loud ululations of joy. With my cousin's permission, I taped the music on the recorder hidden inside the woven bag on my shoulder. The brides wore a fabulous rented white western bridal gown. Gifts came in cash or gold jewelry. According to custom, the bride was heavily adorned with gold jewelry. Singing and feasting lasted into the evening.

Aaron had flown to Israel from Portland, Oregon. My tickets required me to fly back to Western Canada before his return flight to medical school. On our last day together, staying with the Goldenbergs, Tina mentioned that US Secretary of State Warren Christopher was in Jerusalem on a peace mission. Aaron and I filled that day with last minute things I wanted him to see. We had almost reached our last afternoon bus stop to ride home when that bus whizzed right by us. Because of rush hour, I hoped another would come soon, but the posted schedule said it would be thirty minutes.

Meanwhile, we noticed increasing security with police and military presence everywhere. Some raced by on motorcycles, more in cars with flashing lights and shouts in Hebrew. This was the only time I stood at a bus stop in Israel when no one around spoke any language I knew. Our bus did not come in thirty minutes, but a long convoy of roaring motorcycles and police cars did, driving fast, lights flashing and sirens screaming as top security closed the street at both ends.

Finally, a long slow-moving black limousine with Israeli and U.S. flags on fenders rolled by with its passengers waving. They were followed by more police cars and noisy motorcycles. Yes, it was Warren Christopher and staff arriving at the King David Hotel. It was thrilling to be that close to a major event. Aaron and I stood at attention. I have not personally seen greater respect paid to any prominent world leader anywhere than to U.S. Secretary of State, Warren Christopher, on that day—including seeing foreign dignitaries arrive in official processions at Israel's Knesset or national leaders of an African nation touring in Galilee. I felt as if I were seeing a Caesar of ancient Rome, or the leader of the modern free world pass by. I saw and understood that Warren Christopher's power was not his own. I heard these words inwardly, "the power of any ambassador is not in himself, but in the one he represents." That impacted me.

Our bus still didn't come. A young man rode by shouting in Hebrew and a new waiting passenger understood.

"No point waiting," he said. "They've closed this road and routed traffic a different way."

We walked and eventually found our #30 bus. We reached home at 7:40 PM. Tina helped me pack for my 6:25 a.m. bus to Ben Gurion Airport. After warm goodbyes, the ride to Ben Gurion was uneventful. When we reached airport security, they questioned me politely but thoroughly. The airport was quiet. Some concourses were shut and empty. I reached my gate and saw a huge U.S.A. jet waiting outside on the tarmac with special insignia—two flag standards displaying a mix of five large Israeli and U.S. flags each, surrounded by much security. It was Air Force One. I took pictures so Aaron would know I was telling the truth. Soon a motorcycle cavalcade roared into view with soldiers, police as yesterday's top security routine repeated. In the middle of this flurry came Warren Christopher's long black limousine. As I viewed the same impressive cavalcade as the day before, I again heard, "The authority of any ambassador does not rest in himself, but in the power of the one he represents." Today's repeated object lesson powerfully drove the point home.

I enjoyed watching this greatest show of earthly power I'd ever seen. Warren Christopher courteously helped his wife up the boarding ramp. I saw him turn and give confident jaunty waves, saw his attractive secretary-aide in an emerald-green dress, briefcase in hand, dash down the same ramp to give authentic left-right kisses to the cheeks of visiting Arab and Israeli dignitaries, saw secret service men dressed in suits (wearing shoulder holsters) on this hot day ascend both plane ramps backwards, scanning for threats before they went inside as the big plane doors swung shut.

It was time to board my Olympic Airlines plane for Greece. My seat had been assigned weeks ago. Unbelievably, my seat gave me a bird's eye view of the presidential plane. Our jets roared and its jets roared. We taxied down the tarmac parallel to the U.S. plane doing the same, both gaining speed. Our plane took off, mine heading west toward Athens while Warren Christopher's plane veered northeast for his next meeting in Damascus.

But that wasn't the end of my incredible experience. My flight to London let me spend two days with friends before my return flight to Canada. My hostess took me to Cheam Village, Surrey, to catch the bus that would reach Heathrow for a cost of £1.65 versus £17 for a cab, a savings of $32 Canadian then. A rail strike would start that afternoon. I had no idea it would affect bus schedules.

Heather and I chatted as the bus arrived, so I didn't notice it was packed. An older woman had arrived at the stop after me, but since I had luggage, I let her move past me to board first.

However, the driver saw my suitcase and shocked both of us by pointing to me but telling her, "Ducks, this woman is a visitor in our country and has a plane to catch. I must take her to the airport. I'm sorry, but I need to ask you to get off and wait for the next coach in thirty minutes." The startled woman did as she was told.

Once on board, I saw passengers wedged all the way to the back, but I found one empty seat to sit. As we whizzed past other stops where people waited, the driver waved at each group, letting them know he could not stop. I marveled that I was the last person to get on the bus. Without me knowing I needed help, help had been provided for like I was an ambassador on assignment. I think angels were involved.

We reached Heathrow at noon. In pre 9/11 days, Air Canada had said that a one-hour advance check-in time was enough. However, an unbelievable crowd snaked in front of the airline desk. I reached check-in at 1:20 p.m. The plane was scheduled to leave at 1:30. The attendant told me to rush to gate 28. I had no idea how far that was. However, as soon as I dashed through the first departure hallway, an Air Canada female employee on a golf cart flagged me and one older lady down and told us to hop on. At top speed, honking loudly, we passed many people hurrying to other planes and finally reached gate 28 at the end of a very long corridor. We entered the plane's doors at 1:28 p.m., the very last two people to board. Even our luggage made it.

I experienced no worry. I had exceptional help every step of the way—even before I knew I needed it—every bit as good as Warren Christopher's police and military cavalcade. I also felt like an ambassador on assignment and have never had a stronger sense of being protected and provided for.

## Religious Events

**Judaism**—The Bible instructed the Jewish people to go up to Jerusalem three times a year to celebrate the three major feasts.

Believe me, Jerusalem's traffic on those dates proves that they still fully observe those feasts.

**Passover (Pesach)** or the **Feast of Unleavened Bread** commemorates the Israelites leaving slavery in Egypt to journey to the Promised Land. As told in Exodus 12, they packed and left so fast, there was not time for yeast to rise in their bread dough. Unleavened bread (matzot) is a reminder of their hurried exodus. Although not all Jewish people practice their religion, over ninety percent do celebrate Passover each year. Besides doing fabulous cooking, most Jewish wives and mothers delight in cleaning their homes until no dust remains. Some even do a white gloves test.

**The Feast of Weeks or Shavuot/Pentecost** comes fifty days after Passover. Initially a harvest festival, it also honors the giving of the Law or Torah on Mount Sinai. It comes fifty days after the second day of Passover. For Christians, that marks fifty days after Easter resurrection Sunday and the descent of the Holy Spirit on the Apostles and the 120 believers waiting in the Upper Room for the gift of the Holy Spirit as described in Acts, chapter 2.

**Yom Kippur** (also known as the Day of Atonement) is the holiest day of the year for those of the Jewish faith. Each year, it is marked by fasting, prayer, and a reflection on one's sins. It signals the end of the

Ten Days of Awe, a time of repentance following the biblical Feast of Trumpets, which is also the time that Jews mark their civil Jewish New Year, Rosh Hashanah.

**The Feast of Tabernacles or Booths** is the third major yearly feast calling Israel's people to go up to Jerusalem to worship. Its Hebrew name is Sukkot (shelter) and it commemorates their journey through the wilderness to the Promised Land when they built and camped in temporary shelters along the way. As a reminder of God's care, each fall the Jewish people build outdoor booths in courtyards or on rooftops made from the branches of palms, willow, and fruitful boughs. Then they feast inside and spend quality family time together. It is also known as the Festival of Ingathering or the Feast of Tabernacles.

**Purim**—This joyful springtime festival celebrates the deliverance of the Jewish people through Queen Esther's courage and obedience. When wicked Haman tried to annihilate the Jews, his plans were reversed upon his and his own sons' heads. Part of the Purim observance includes reading the book of Esther aloud. Each time Haman's name is said, hearers use noisemakers to blot it out and symbolically defeat him.

**Chanukah/Hanukkah** is the joyous eight-day celebration observed by adding and lighting one candle each night until all eight are burning. Also known as the Feast of Renewal or Feast of Light, it celebrates the Maccabean victory over the Seleucid/Syrian Army when only a one-day supply of oil was available to keep the menorah alight 'in Jerusalems rededicated Temple, but God miraculously multiplied that one-day supply to keep the lamp burning for eight days. Therefore, the Hanukkah is celebrated for eight days.

Other important Israeli celebrations include Independence Day, Memorial Day, and Holocaust Day.

**Easter** and **Christmas** dates on the Christian calendar are times when many additional events are celebrated via processions and/or other church observances.

**Major Islamic Observances**

**Ramadan** is the most sacred month of the year for Muslims, the month when they believe that all scripture was revealed to Mohammed. He taught, "When the month of Ramadan starts, the gates of heaven are opened and the gates of hell are closed and the devils are chained." Muslims fast from dawn to sunset each day through the month as a spiritual discipline to contemplate their relationship with God, have time for extra prayer, increased charity, and Quran study, but it's also a time of joyful celebration and gift giving. It ends with Eid al-Fitr, a three-day Festival that means The Breaking of the Fast.

**Eid al-Adha**, Islam's other major feast, is celebrated on the tenth day of the last month in their calendar. It marks the peak of the annual Hajj pilgrimage to Mecca and commemorates God appearing to Ibrahim/Abraham in a dream commanding that he sacrifice his son, Ishmael, as an act of obedience. There is no mention of Isaac. Jews and Christians also honor this event of when God miraculously provided a substitute.

Details regarding pilgrimages, tours, services, concerts, and more are easily found online. Here are some to consider:

- Passover Seder
- Easter services at the Church of the Holy Sepulcher
- Easter at the Garden Tomb
- Palm Sunday and Good Friday processions
- Ramadan and Eid celebrations and observances
- Hanukkah/Chanukah celebrations and observances
- Church of the Nativity, Bethlehem, offers masses on Christmas Eve as well as on many other special occasions during the year.
- Churches and Christian sites around the Sea of Galilee, including the beautiful new Boat Chapel at Magdala, as well as the Church of the Transfiguration at the top of Mount Tabor, offer frequent tours and special masses and services.

Many more locations also celebrate regular or special masses and services. Check their websites for specific dates and times.

**Things to Do**

- Do follow your schedule. Be where you say you will be when expected and on time. Have contact information available so you can phone if you experience transportation breakdown or any inadvertent delay.

**Things Not To Do**

- Do not abandon schedules or cause inconvenience and consternation to the people scheduled to serve and interact with you.

# 6

## OFF THE BEATEN PATH

HIDDEN GEMS AND RECOMMENDED TOURS AND ORGANIZATIONS

Here is my list of top recommended interesting and fun places to enjoy as time allows.

**Galilee**—Along with the traditional sites associated with Jesus's ministry, don't miss newly developed Magdala at Migdal Junction near Tiberias.

**Christ Church Guest House**, Coffee House, Museum, church, and more are the compound next to the post office near Jaffa Gate in the heart of Jerusalem's Old City. Delicious meals may be arranged in advance with those managing the Guest House. It is great food served by a kind staff at good prices that also provides great visiting and networking opportunities. Find information at https://www.cmj-israel.org/christ-church-guest-house

**The Biblical Gardens at Yad Hashmona** west of Jerusalem in the scenic Judean hills. The community and its history are fascinating.

The **Elvis American Café** on the north side of the Jerusalem Tel-Aviv Highway at Abu Ghosh. The 16-foot Elvis statue marks this 1950s-style diner next to a large gas station. Travelers will enjoy good American and Middle Eastern food at reasonable prices but the strongest draw is the biggest collection of Elvis photographs and memorabilia outside of North America. Diners hear Elvis croon songs in the background on a continuous loop. This fun and unique tribute is far from his hometown of Tupelo, Mississippi. They also serve good ice cream.

**Trezoro Restaurant in Ein Kerem** is famous for excellent frozen yogurt and Italian ice creams. Those traveling with me raved about the many flavor choices.

**The small fruit and vegetable market** across the main street from Trezoro in Ein Kerem has a personable proprietor. Visit, enjoy, and buy from him. The last time we visited, his son had just been called up to active IDF duty and we discussed the realities of war.

**Small shops in Ein Kerem** on narrow roads going uphill to the cathedral from the main street offer (mostly) good merchandise at fair prices. However, don't pay the initial price asked. They expect you to bargain. You will usually be pleased with the final prices.

In Ein Kerem one shopkeeper recommended The Mala Bistro at the foot of the hill on the main street and we were pleased. They offered delicious authentic foods in great atmosphere.

**The Lebanon Café at 88 Kvish ha-Shalom in Abu Ghosh** specializes in authentic Lebanese foods. They offer a wide variety of dishes in a pleasant atmosphere at moderate prices. Free parking is available across the street.

**The Abu Ghosh Restaurant** owned by Jaodat Ibrahim is world famous for preparing the Guinness World Record largest dish of hummus in a satellite dish measuring 20 feet (6.1 m), weighing 8992.5 pounds (4,087.5 kg.), nearly twice the size of the previous record set in Beirut, Lebanon. See the celebration and hear the music at https://www.youtube.com/watch?v=gt2bszXkeN4 and https://www.youtube.com/watch?v=Llt47P3o9cI

**St. Peter's fish** is a form of tilapia served at restaurants and kibbutzes everywhere throughout Galilee. Named for the fisherman disciple, it is a delicacy to enjoy while in the area if visitors like fish at all. Kibbutz Nof Ginosar operates fish farms to replenish local stock. That is also where paying a small fee lets visitors see the two-thousand-year-old Jesus Boat found nearby when water levels were low. It is preserved in the kibbutz's museum.

**Sea of Galilee boat tours** ensure beautiful views and are well worth the money. My favorite is Daniel's Worship Boat, which you can find online.

**Beersheba's Camel Market** In 2017, after a century of operation, Be'er Sheva closed the city's open-air Bedouin market. Its closure boosts business at other city markets, but I do not know how bride prices are arranged and paid these days.

**Kibbutzes/Kibbutzim**—stop to visit at least one of these bold early settlements which were originally collective communities based on agriculture, whether you spend a night in the well-maintained guest houses many offer, eat in restaurants, and/or see their interesting arts/crafts/and foods gift shops.

## Recommended Tours, Organizations, YouTube Features

The Galilee Experience https://www.youtube.com/watch?v=WO221GpZiQY

Arie Bar David—an outstanding tour guide and Israeli hero. You can find many of his worthwhile posts online, especially on YouTube. One is Yad Hashmona–Memory of the Eight but search out others as well.

I consider Sar-El Tours the best https://sareltours.com/ Hoshen Blvd 5, Mevaseret Zion, 9074020 Israel Phone: +972 2-533-8000.

## Things to Do

- Do take time to stroll the streets and, when there's opportunity, visit with residents and shop proprietors.
- If you buy souvenirs or keepsakes, bargain politely in the spirit of fun. It is an expected and usually enjoyable art form in Israel and many other countries. Several times when I haven't liked an item enough to settle on a price offered, I've walked away but shopkeepers have pursued me with the item in a bag eager to close the sale, and so far

I've always accepted. However, we usually agree in the shop with both the seller and buyer wearing happy smiles.

**Things Not to Do**

- Be polite and friendly but not too personal or probing in discussions with Israeli residents (or with people anywhere).

# 7

# HEADING HOME

**Special Keepsakes**

Many tourist sites sell things like water from the River Jordan, the Dead Sea, the Sea of Galilee, or even the Mediterranean. I prefer to buy Israeli bottled water to drink and then fill the empty plastic bottles with the special waters I want to bring back from destinations like the Jordan River or Dead Sea for myself and friends.

These are typically small amounts of liquid so not a problem at airport security, though they need to be in checked luggage and it's wise to check your particular airline's requirements. Seashells, rocks, pebbles, sand, etc., are other great keepsakes to make into jewelry, other various souvenir items, or simply to keep for display.

The same is true of Israeli coins, even the ones no longer in circulation are found inexpensively in Israeli thrift or antique shops. One shop in particular sits on an easily-accessed corner in the Old City's Jewish Quarter where I visit every time, sort through the merchandise, and usually leave with treasures.

I don't generally drink sodas but do save empty Coke or other pop cans from countries I visit. After removing the tops, these make great souvenir containers to store and display items such as ancient mosaic or pottery fragments, interesting shells, rocks, salt crystals, sand, coins—anything meaningful from those nations.

The language of the writing on the can's label identifies where the items were found.

Gathering and preserving flowers, herbs, leaves, and similar items from areas where it's legal to collect them (*not* national parks) is another good way to remember trip highlights. I have loved cooking with bay leaves from Ravenna, Italy or rosemary from Jerusalem where it grows abundantly including often as lane dividers in some streets and highways. When traffic stalled on the way back from the Garden of Gethsemane and we were hungry, I reached through my open driver's window and picked fresh rosemary for my passengers to nibble on or bring home.

Excellent books are available that identify Israel's Bible era and current plants, trees, animals, and more. Beautiful artworks, ceramics, glassware, and jewelry in all price points are excellent purchases to bring home, along with countless other appealing items. Purchases don't need to be expensive to create happy, lasting memories.

## Departing Flights

For international flights, do arrive two to three hours early for check-in as recommended at most airports—longer than what is specified at airports like Barajas in Madrid where I found things very complicated. At Ninoy Aquino International Airport in Manila, Philippines, as well as at Ben Gurion International near Tel Aviv, secure check-in really does require the full three hours stated. In fact, I usually add a little time to that.

## Things To Do

- Do pack luggage wisely so nothing delays you at customs. Agricultural products must be sealed for export. For

example, ram's horn shofars bought for souvenirs are inspected as to their agricultural source, etc.
- Do have the names and addresses handy of people you have visited in Israel or places you've stayed as that is usually asked by customs officers before your departure.
- Do have receipts accessible and if you have bought generously, allow time to get your VAT refund unless the particular places you shopped did not add the VAT tax, which is happening more often than it used to.
- Do arrive at the airport for the full amount of advance time suggested for your flight.

**Things Not To Do**

- Do not pack sharp or dangerous items in your carry-on luggage unless you are willing to have them confiscated.
- Do not ever leave luggage unattended or carry items for others without knowing what they are and personally doing the packing.
- Do not tease or engage in loose talk mentioning terrorism if you wish to make your flight. On the day Cindy and I explored Baal Hazor, I basically had sunstroke and slurred my words. Proud of following Tina's guidelines to fit in, when boarding a public bus, I said to Cindy, "We don't look like tourists, do we?" but it sounded like, "We don't look like terrorists…." I don't like drinking soda but since we had run out of water, Cindy made me drink soda until my speech returned somewhat to normal.

# 8

## KEEPING ISRAEL ALIVE WITH YOU

When I returned from my first wonderful lengthy trip to Israel, I did all I could to keep my connections with people in that country close and alive. I wrote letters and made occasional phone calls when I could afford them (pre-WhatsApp). I subscribed to The Jerusalem Post daily newspaper and several other daily, weekly, or monthly publications online daily at relatively low cost and enjoyed them.

It's easier these days. Almost countless close connection opportunities are available. Facebook didn't exist when I first visited Israel or WhatsApp or Zoom or a myriad of other applications that let us see and chat with or buy from people as if we're in the same room. It's also possible to take virtual tours of desired destinations, events, and much more.

Those are great substitutes for the real thing. However, when possible, there's nothing like walking the land for yourself, seeing the colors and panoramas, touching ancient stones, letting desert sands slip through our fingers, boating, floating or swimming in amazing waters, breathing in the smells, or eating the sun-drenched foods with Israeli locals, etc.

# 9

# ISRAEL'S WONDERFUL BEST-LOVED FOODS AND RECIPES

Kosher is the term applied to the food or facility in which food is sold or prepared to fulfill the requirements of Jewish law as stated in Leviticus and Deuteronomy. Kosher kitchens contain two completely separate sinks and food preparation stations for meat and dairy products with utensils for each. Orthodox and Reformed families own and use separate dishes, glassware, silverware, etc., for both meat and dairy.

In stores, Kosher foods are identified by labels showing "meat," "dairy," or "neutral." The letter "P" denotes Parve, meaning it contains no meat or dairy. Four regulating agencies use these following symbols to identify Kosher: OU, Kof-K, OK, and Star-K.

Jewish commercial food laws require that meat and dairy not be served or eaten together in the same meal. For example, if someone orders a McDonald's hamburger in Israel, my son Aaron found the accompanying milkshake was made from a soy product, not dairy milk. A MacDavid fast food restaurant (sometimes spelled McDavid) began in Tel Aviv in 1978. After expanding to twenty-eight branches, only one in Haifa remains open today.

There is a kosher McDonald's in Jerusalem and another in Mevesseret Zion, a suburb west of Jerusalem.

**Rich cultural experience is gained through enjoying local and national foods**

Travelers need to eat and usually enjoy trying new dishes. I have journeyed in lands where it was not wise to ask questions about what we were eating or how it was prepared. At times during my three and a half months in the jungles of Colombia, South America in the 1980's, I did not always like the answers. No matter where travelers go in Israel, enjoying the foods grown and the cuisine prepared is a memorable and wonderful part of the trip.

The Bible promised that Israel would be a land of milk and honey, of grapes, pomegranates, figs, dates, olives, and flowing streams, where the earth would give its fruits, and the desert "would blossom like a rose." Since early times, the nation's farmers, citizens and scientists, have worked hard to make that promise come true. Today Israelis are among the world's leading experts on drip irrigation, desalinization, crop germination, grafting, and many other related skills that make the land excel in fruits, vegetables, grains, flowers, meat and dairy production, and much more.

Visit Israel's markets. A walk through Jerusalem's huge downtown Mahane Yehuda market, or similar food and produce markets anywhere in the country is an almost-religious experience. The sights, smells, tastes, feels, textures, and more, show the Bible's promises of abundance have come true.

Delicious honey-drenched candies and desserts are available in open-air shops for a few shekels, and these days coffee shops are almost everywhere. The secret to obtaining something close to the robust brewed coffee many North Americans prefer is to request an Americano with a dash of cold milk. Otherwise, if you just order coffee, you will usually get a latté. It's fun to sample the variety of ways coffee is made and served in Israel.

On my early visits to Israel, American style brewed coffee is what I missed most. Coffee there then was made from packets of instant powdered Nescafé, sometimes with sugar and powdered creamer already added. There were no coffee shops. On my third trip, I was in downtown Tel Aviv one day when someone strolled by carrying a take-out cup with the delicious aroma of brewed coffee. I literally followed the person until I caught up to ask where they had purchased such a delight. It is easy these days to find fairly good coffee. One favorite Airbnb in Jerusalem came equipped with a Keurig and assorted coffee pods. The host at our 2023 Airbnb in Arbel in the Galilee brewed wonderful lattes or Americanos for us each free each morning. We could have ordered more at other times if desired. That is all appreciated progress!

In Israel, our eyes feast on the colors, fragrances, textures, and new and bigger varieties of all manner of things sold in the open-air markets where every stand is piled high with delights like the Garden of Eden. And nothing is very expensive. We bought seven large ripe avocados for ten shekels, $3.50 US, and then examined many selections of breads, cheeses, hummus, fruit and nut-nougat candies, amid several city blocks worth of aisles and booths. Most vendors allow shoppers to taste samples before buying.

My next trip to Israel coincided with the eight-day religious holiday of Succoth or the fall Feast of Booths. That is when people celebrate their coming out of Egypt into the Promised Land by erecting shelters of woven branches in yards or on rooftops or hotel courtyards, all decorated with the proper varieties of fruits and lights in an atmosphere of gift giving and celebration much like Christmas. Families spend as much time as they can together, usually eating and sleeping in the shelters, while thanking God and celebrating family.

Israelis are known to cook some of the most delicious and possibly the healthiest foods on the planet. As a result, the majority enjoy impressively good health and longevity. Friends who go there with me rave about Israel's tasty, healthy dishes that we get hungry for after we leave. We collect recipes and perfect them until we get together again to recreate the foods we enjoyed in Tel Aviv, Jerusalem, Beersheba, Tiberias, or Qumran.

Here, I'm pleased to list some of Israel's most representative and best-loved foods. Rich cultural experience is shared through preparing, cooking, eating, and enjoying national and local foods, especially when that experience is enjoyed with local people.

As mentioned, a walk through any Farmers Market in Israel shows an amazing variety of fruits and vegetables—many I've found nowhere else. I love licorice-flavored anise that grows wild in many locations. I break off a piece to chew and enjoy its flavor. Rosemary grows in garden hedges and in roadway medians. Capers grow in the cracks between the massive limestone blocks in the Western Wall as well as almost everywhere else and are often pickled to add their special taste to salads and other dishes.

Many Middle Eastern dishes use traditional natural ingredients that have been available for hundreds of years. They are named in the recipes below, but substitutions are also acceptable.

In Old City's bakeries or markets, enjoy a **Boureka** fresh from the oven. These flaky pastries come in a wide variety of savory fillings, typically cheese, potatoes, or spinach.

**Falafel** is one of Israel's national dishes. Chefs in Israel and around the world acknowledge Falafel as a unique Middle Eastern Arab dish. The recipe is available on picture postcards everywhere in Israel. Made from deep fried chickpea or garbanzo bean balls slipped into pita bread, these are served with any variety of "salad toppings." The toppings typically include lettuce, cilantro, sliced fresh (or pickled) peppers, cabbage, eggplant, olives, onions, cauliflower, diced tomatoes, and cucumbers, with tahini (sesame) sauce. Falafel is a delicious low-cost high protein dish loved everywhere in the nation.

**Knafeh** is a traditional Middle Eastern dessert that's not excessively sweet. Made with shredded wheat or pastry noodles covered with sweetened sheep or goat cheese, Knafeh is usually seared and caramelized on both sides and topped with a simple syrup blended with crushed pistachios.

**Shawarma** is another national favorite of Jewish and Arab people. Originally lamb or mutton, shawarma today also includes chicken, turkey, beef, or veal roasted on a slowly turning vertical rotisserie or spit. The cooked meat is shaved into thin slices and served.

Rich cultural experience is shared through preparing, cooking, eating, and enjoying regional and national foods, especially when that experience is enjoyed with local people. Rather than sharing a great many of Israel's best loved recipes here, I'm providing a representative list of favorites you can easily find online with cooking instructions and illustrations. In no particular order below, I've listed tried and true well-loved dishes worth your attention.

- Alo Gobi
- Baba Ghanoush Maklubeh
- Pomegranate Feta Salad Apple Fig Walnut Bread Olive Bread
- Basic Bagels Jerusalem Bagels Za'atar
- Date-filled Cookies Date Paste or Spread
- Anise Seed Cookies—Arabic Biscotti Anise Rings (Kaak Be-Yansoon) Arabic Anise Cookies
- Grated Beet Salad Hummus (Chick Pea Paste)
- Halva or Sesame Seed-Honey Candy Varieties Shakshuka
- Tabouli/Tabbouleh Tahini

**ALO GOBI**
(Popular in Israel and Jordan)*
1 lb. cauliflower, separated into florets
4 large, unpeeled potatoes cut into quarters.
2 Tbsp. oil
1/2 tsp. cumin seeds
1 tsp. garlic, minced
2 green hot peppers cut into strips
1 tsp. fresh ginger, cut into thin strips
1 onion cut into strips.
2 tomatoes, chopped
1/2 tsp. salt
1/2 tsp. turmeric
1/2 tsp. ground cumin
1/2 tsp. ground red chili or sweet paprika
1 Tbsp. fresh cilantro, chopped

1/2 tsp. dried mango powder or 1/2 tsp. lemon juice

**Directions**

1. Cook potatoes and cauliflower in saltwater 10 minutes. Drain and set aside.

2. Heat oil in frying pan. Add cumin seeds and sauté a few seconds. Add garlic and ginger, stirring briefly.

3. Add hot pepper, onion, and tomatoes and cook 5 minutes.

4. Add potatoes, cauliflower, turmeric, and cumin. Mix well, cover, and cook 5 minutes.

5. Sprinkle mango powder or lemon juice on top. Stir and remove from heat. Garnish with cilantro.

\* Barry & Batya Segal

---

## BABA GHANOUSH\*

This roasted eggplant dish blended with lemon juice, tahini (sesame paste), and sea salt is a flavorful variation of Hummus.

Typically, the eggplant is grilled over the flame of a grill or gas stove. Slicing the eggplant into rounds and broiling it is another way to achieve the desired roasted flavor that takes less time and many consider it as delicious as the traditional method.

Another option is to roast the eggplant slices in the oven. For maximum caramelized flavor, slice the eggplant in half and roast it at 450 F for 35-40 minutes until the purple skin pulls away from the flesh and pulp. Scoop out the contents and blend by hand or mixer until smooth, although typically the dish has some texture. Eggplant is amazingly nutritious.

\*Victoria Quintero Eaton

## MAKLUBEH

Maklubeh is a traditional dish of Israel and Jordan. It includes meat, rice, and fried vegetables cooked in a pot which is flipped upside down when served, earning the name maklubeh, which means "upside-down."

The dish may include any variety of vegetables, such as fried tomatoes, potatoes, cauliflower, eggplant, and chicken or lamb. When the casserole is inverted, the top is bright red from the tomatoes that now form the top layer and cover the eggplant.

Maklubeh is typically served with yogurt or a salad of diced tomato, cucumber, parsley, and lemon juice, often mixed with tahini sauce.

2 large onions, thinly sliced.
Oil for frying
1 1/4 lbs. lamb, cut into 1/2" pieces
Salt and pepper
1 tsp. allspice
1 tsp. cardamom
Pinch of cloves
1 cauliflower divided into florets
2 eggplants sliced into 1/2 inch rounds, salted, rinsed, and dried
1 1/4 lbs. rice

**Directions**

1. In large, heavy pot, fry onions until translucent. Add the meat and brown.

2. Add water and spices. Then cover and cook over medium heat until tender (about 30 minutes).

3. In a separate pan, fry cauliflower and eggplant until golden.

4. Place a layer of cauliflower over the meat and layer eggplant over the cauliflower.

5. Add rice. Season with salt and cover with water. Do not stir.

6. Simmer, cover, and cook over low heat for 1–1.5 hours until all liquids are absorbed. Turn off heat and keep covered for another 10 minutes.

7. Remove the lid and place a flat platter on the pot. Invert and release the dish onto the platter.

## POMEGRANATE FETA SALAD

This salad is a wonderful blend of salty and sweet flavors from the feta cheese and the pomegranate seeds. Prep. time is 10 minutes.

**Ingredients:**

1/2 C. pecans

1/4 C. sugar

1 (10 ounce) package or good-sized bowl of mixed baby greens 1 pomegranate, peeled, with seeds separated (sometimes these are available in grocery produce sections.)

1/4 red onion, sliced thin

1 (8 ounce) package crumbled feta cheese

**Dressing:**

1 tsp. Dijon mustard

3 Tbsp. red wine vinegar

3 Tbsp. extra-virgin olive oil

1 lemon, zested and juiced

Salt and pepper to taste.

**Directions:**

1. Candy the pecans by placing the sugar in a small skillet and pouring the pecans on top. Cook over medium heat until sugar melts and turns a caramel color, stirring constantly so that the nuts and sugar do not burn. It takes a while for the sugar to start melting, so be patient. Once the sugar turns caramel color, stir to coat the pecans. Pour the pecans onto greased wax paper or aluminum foil to cool. After they cool, break the pecans into pieces.

1. Place the lettuce, pomegranate seeds, red onion, feta cheese, and pecan pieces in a large mixing bowl and set aside. Pomegranate pear salad is another tasty variation.

2. Whisk the Dijon mustard, vinegar, olive oil, lemon zest, lemon juice (to taste), salt, and pepper together in a separate bowl. Pour over the salad and toss to coat. Serve.

**APPLE FIG WALNUT BREAD***

1 ½ cups whole wheat flour 1 tsp. baking soda
1 tsp. cinnamon
¼ tsp. ground nutmeg
⅛ tsp. cloves
⅛ tsp. allspice 2 eggs
½ cups sugar
¼ cup canola oil
¼ cup plain Greek or regular yogurt
¾ cup applesauce
¼ cup fig jam or preserves 1 tsp. vanilla
1 small to medium fresh apple, finely chopped
½ cup walnuts, chopped

**Directions**

1. Preheat oven to 350 F. Spray a 9" X 5" loaf pan with cooking spray.
2. In a small bowl or on a sheet of wax paper sift together the flour, soda, and spices.
3. In a medium or large mixing bowl, whisk together the eggs and sugar, mixing thoroughly. Add the oil, yogurt, applesauce, jam, and vanilla. When well mixed, gradually add the flour ingredients until just combined. Stir in fresh apple and walnuts.
4. Pour batter into loaf pan and cook for 45 minutes or until done.
5. Place baked loaf on a wire rack to cool.

Fresh figs are delicious and healthy. They are also wonderful in preserves and prepared other ways. This recipe uses a small amount of fruit, but the remainder is a great topping on frozen vanilla yogurt or plain Greek or regular yogurt, or many other uses.

*Linda Ross Shoaf

∼

**OLIVE BREAD***

2 large red onions, thinly sliced
2 Tbsp. olive oil

1 1/3 C. pitted black, green with pimento, or any favorite olives
7 C. flour
1 1/2 tsp. salt
4 tsp. dry yeast
3 Tbsp. each parsley and coriander

**Directions**

1. Fry onions in oil until soft. Chop olives coarsely. In a bowl, combine flour, salt, yeast, herbs, olives, and fried onions.

1. Add 2 C. of hand-hot water. Mix into dough. Put on a floured surface and knead for 10 minutes. Let rise until double (about 1 hr.)

2. Shape into two loaves. Make cuts in the top of the loaves. Put them on a greased cookie sheet. Let them double in size. Bake at 425 F. for 40 minutes until the loaves sound hollow when thumped. (Can be shaped into 16 rolls instead if desired which would bake for 25 mins.)

*Ibolya Agoston

∽

## BASIC BAGELS

1 1/4 C. water
4 1/2 C. bread flour
3 Tbsp. white sugar
1 tsp. salt
2 Tbsp. vegetable oil
1 Tbsp. instant yeast.
4 Qts. Water
1 C. honey (optional)
Toppings
2 Tbsp. poppy seeds (optional)
2 Tbsp. sesame seeds (optional
2 Tbsp. dried onion flakes (optional)
1 Tbsp. coarse salt (optional)

**Directions**

1. Combine 1 1/4 C. water, flour, sugar, 1 tsp. salt, vegetable oil, and

yeast in the mixing bowl or in the bowl of a stand mixer. Mix on low speed using the dough hook for around 8 minutes.

2. To be sure the gluten has developed, cut off a small piece of dough. Flour your fingers to stretch the dough. If it tears easily, the dough needs more kneading. When ready, the dough should form a thin clear "window."

3. Transfer the dough to a lightly oiled bowl. Cover it with plastic wrap and a towel. Let rise for 2 hours.

4. Punch down the dough. Place it on a lightly floured board and use a knife to divide the dough into six pieces (or more for smaller bagels). Roll each piece of dough into a sausage shape about 6 inches long. Join the ends to form a circle. Repeat with the remaining dough. Let the bagels rest for 15 minutes.

5. Preheat oven to 475 degrees F. Line a baking sheet with parchment paper. Fill small bowls with poppy seeds, sesame seeds, and onion flakes.

6. Bring 4 Qts. water to a boil in a large pot. Add honey, if desired. Boil the bagels, three at a time, until they rise to the water's surface, about 1 minute per side.

7. Remove the bagels with a slotted spoon and place them on the parchment-lined baking sheet.

8. Dip the tops of the wet bagels into the toppings and arrange them, seeds up, on the baking sheet. Sprinkle with coarse salt, if desired. Bake in the preheated oven until the bagels begin to brown, 15 to 20 minutes.

∼

## JERUSALEM BAGELS

I didn't know the correct name for these until I researched recipes. I know and love these from buying them from street vendors in Old City Jerusalem. I assumed they were an Arab bread because they are served with delicious Za'atar spice, but this is the name in recipe books. I am delighted to find and share this favorite which I now make and enjoy at home.

4 1/4 C. all-purpose flour
3/4-ounce fresh yeast or 3 1/2 tsp. active dry yeast
1 C. milk plus 1/2 C. water, heated together until warm
1/4 C. neutral-flavored oil, such as sunflower
3 Tbsp. sugar
1 beaten egg
1/2 C. sesame seeds
2 Tbsp. sugar

**Directions:**

1. Place the yeast in a large bowl with the water/milk mixture, oil, and sugar. Stir gently and cover the bowl. Allow the yeast to activate for 10 minutes. If using a mixer, use the mixer bowl.

2. Whisk the yeast mixture together to disperse lumps. Sift the flour over the liquid and mix vigorously. If using a mixer, fit the dough hook and mix for 10 minutes. If kneading by hand, knead for 10 minutes. Either way, the dough should be smooth and slightly tacky.

3. Cover the bowl with plastic wrap or a recycled plastic bag and allow it to rise for 30 minutes or until doubled in size.

4. Sprinkle your work surface with flour. Divide the dough into sixths. Roll each piece into one long roll about 1 1/2 feet long.

5. Join and press the ends together. Hook a forefinger into the bottom of the hole that you made and gently stretch the dough to make a long oblong hole.

6. Preheat the oven to 350° degrees F. Line two baking trays with baking parchment.

7. Place the bagels on trays with the joined side down. Brush with the beaten egg, turning the tray to reach all sides of the bagels. It is important to coat the bagels at this point and not wait until they are ready to bake, because then they will be light and fragile and may collapse under the brush.

8. In a small bowl, mix the sesame seeds and sugar. Sprinkle generously over the bagels, again turning the tray to ensure that the maximum surface area is covered with the seed/sugar mix. Sesame seeds give this bagel its wonderful characteristic flavor.

## ZA'ATAR

Za'atar is called "brain food" because of its antioxidant and medicinal qualities. Recipes vary greatly (some are guarded family secrets). This one is made with ingredients normally found in most kitchens. One exception is sumac which is bright, pinkish red, with a tart, almost lemony flavor.

1 Tbsp. dried thyme-crushed
1 Tbsp. ground cumin
1 Tbsp. ground coriander
1 Tbsp. toasted sesame seeds
1 Tbsp. sumac
1/2 tsp. Kosher salt
1/4 tsp. or more chili flakes-optional

**Directions:**

Mix all ingredients together in a small bowl. Store in an airtight container.

For the best flavor, toast whole seeds (cumin, coriander, and sesame seeds) until fragrant and then grind. Za'atar is delicious on breads or sprinkled on hummus, but is also great served with any of the following:

Cauliflower
Cucumber
Eggplant
Fennel
Feta and other cheeses
Fresh leafy herbs (parsley, mint, cilantro, etc.)
Lemon or lime
Pistachios Pita bread
Potatoes
Olive oil and olives
Quinoa
Rice
Tomato

Watermelon
Yogurt

~

**DATE-FILLED COOKIES**

These melt-in-your-mouth date-filled cookies are low in sugar but rich in flavor. I first enjoyed them in an Arab home in East Jerusalem on my first trip to Israel and have searched for the recipe ever since—I'm very glad to have found it!

Dough yields 20 x 2 inch cookies.

1/4 C. milk slightly heated, but not enough to kill the yeast.

1/4 tsp. active dry yeast

2 C. unbleached all-purpose flour

1 Tbsp. sugar

2 Tbsp. canola oil

6 Tbsp. melted butter

1/2 tsp. pure vanilla extract

1/4 C. water

**Directions**

1. In a small bowl, mix the milk and yeast. Set aside until the yeast softens and is foamy, 3-5 minutes.

2. In a medium bowl, mix flour and sugar together.

3. Rub the oil and melted butter into the flour with your fingertips until the mixture is a sandy texture.

4. Add the yeast, milk mixture, and vanilla, mixing gently.

5. Add water a small bit at a time, mixing gently after each addition, until this forms a soft dough.

6. Cover the dough and let it rest for 10 minutes while you prepare the filling.

**Filling**

4 oz. chopped pitted dates

1 1/2 tsp. canola oil

1/8 tsp. pure almond extract

1/4 tsp. cinnamon

1/8 tsp. ground cardamom

Pinch of anise

**Directions:**

1. Place the chopped dates in a small saucepan along with the other filling ingredients.

2. Cover the saucepan and heat medium heat 7-10 minutes, stirring occasionally, until the dates soften like jam.

3. Preheat oven to 350 F. Separate the dough into 1 Tbsp. portions. Roll each into a ball.

4. Flatten each dough ball into a disc and place 1 tsp. of filling in its center. Fold the dough edges around the filling; crimp them together to seal in the filling.

5. Roll the filled cookie gently between your hands to regain the ball shape. Then, flatten the cookie slightly.

6. Place the filled cookies onto a parchment-lined baking sheet 1" apart. Bake 25 minutes, rotating the baking sheet once during baking. Remove the cookies when they are a light golden brown. Cool before dusting with powdered sugar.

7. They may be stored in an airtight container for 2-3 weeks (if your family doesn't eat them first).

Adapted from (Maamoul) https://www.curiouscuisiniere.com/maamoul-cookies/

The Prophet Muhammad is quoted as saying, "When one of you is fasting, he should break his fast with dates; but if he cannot get any, then he should break his fast with water, for water is purifying." Dates are a Middle East staple symbolizing abundance and rich in fiber, potassium, and calcium to help keep the body healthy. That's one reason why Ma'amoul, date-filled cookies, are a delicious and favorite part of this celebration.

∼

**DATE PASTE OR SPREAD**

Dates are also wonderful prepared in a simple process making date paste or spread. In form and texture, it compares with North

American apple butter. It is a delicious treat by itself or spread on rolls, breads, cakes, or anything. It is an excellent sugar substitute in baking. Best of all, its preparation is simple.

Bring 1 quart of water to a low boil.

Remove from heat. Soak 12 oz. of dates in the water. Let them swell as the water cools.

Drain the dates but save 1 C. of the water they soaked in. Combine the dates and 1 C. of water in a high-speed blender. Blend until smooth.

Store the date paste or spread in a clean covered container. Refrigerate once it is opened.

## ANISE SEED COOKIES—ARABIC BISCOTTI

2 1/2 C. flour

1 Tbsp. baking powder

Pinch of salt

1 C. sugar

2-3 Tbsp. powdered Anise (yansoon)

3 tsp. vanilla

3 large eggs

1/3 C. vegetable oil

1/2 C. slivered almonds

**Directions**

1. Mix the eggs, sugar, and vanilla and beat well. Add oil and anise/yansoon. Mix well.

2. Mix all dry ingredients and sift them over the wet ingredients. The dough should be stiff and hard to spread. If it spreads easily, add more flour.

3. Lightly rub oil on the palm of your hands. Separate the dough into two or three parts and shape into logs on your baking sheet, as if you were making regular biscotti 1-1.5 inches high as they will rise slightly. Make each log the same size so they cook evenly.

4. Pre-heat oven to 350 F and bake for 20 minutes. Remove from

oven and cool slightly before slicing into bars and placing each bar on its side. Flip each bar to the other side and bake for another 5-7 minutes until crisp and a golden color.

5. Sprinkle almonds on top and serve or store.

## ANISE RINGS (KAAK BE-YANSOON)

This recipe makes 45 anise rings 2" in diameter.

2 tsp. baking powder
2 large eggs
2 Tbsp. milk powder
2 Tbsp. anise seeds
1 Tbsp. ground anise seeds
1 C. vegetable oil or melted butter or margarine (or a mixture of both)
2 1/2 C. all-purpose flour Dough will be stiff
2 1/2 C. flour
1 Tbsp. baking powder Pinch of salt
1 C. sugar
2-3 Tbsp. powdered Anise (Yansoon)
3 tsp. vanilla
3 large or 4 medium eggs
1/3 C. vegetable oil
1/2 C. slivered almonds

**Directions**

1. Mix and beat the eggs, sugar, and vanilla. Add oil and anise/yansoon and mix well.

2. Mix all dry ingredients and sift them over the wet ingredients.

Many Middle Eastern recipes use natural ingredients that have been available for hundreds of years and are available in most Middle-Eastern markets. These cookies are flavored with the seeds of sesame, anise, kazha, and mahlep.

## ARABIC ANISE COOKIES

(another popular variation)

4 C. flour

1 C. sugar

1 C. toasted sesame seeds

4 tsp. baking powder

2 Tbsp whole anise seed

2 tsp. kazha, also called black seed or Nigella sativa. They look like black sesame seeds and have a slightly pungent bitter taste.

1/2 tsp mahlep (or mahlab) powder is an aromatic spice made from the St Lucie cherry. The stones are cracked to extract the seed, which is soft and chewy. The seed is ground to powder before being used. Its flavor is similar to that of bitter almond and cherry, and also to marzipan. However, 1/2 tsp of almond extract may be substituted.

1 C. vegetable oil (canola)

1 C. water

**Directions**

1. Preheat the oven to 350°F. Mix all dry ingredients together. Add the vegetable oil and mix until the ingredients start to form a sandy mixture.

2. While mixing, slowly add water (approximately one cup) until the dough has enough moisture to be shaped into small balls or bars about an inch thick. Meatball tongs or a small ice cream scoop may be used to form the cookies.

3. Place the formed balls on a baking sheet and bake until the bottoms of the cookies start to brown, about 20 minutes. Turn the cookies over to bake for an additional 15 minutes to get a crisp center.

4. Cool and store them in an air-tight container. You may also shape them into small rings.

## COUSCOUS TOMATO CUCUMBER SALAD

Couscous are little toasted balls of semolina flour. The main ingredients here are couscous and equal amounts of sliced cherry or regular tomatoes and unpeeled cucumbers. I garnish with parsley. Other possible additions can be chives or mint added to the bowl along with the cucumbers, tomatoes, and couscous, giving it all a good mix. Feta cheese and/or tuna may be added for flavor and extra protein if desired.

∼

**GRATED BEET SALAD**
   2 Tbsp. rice vinegar
   Juice from 1/2 lime
   Pinches of sugar, salt, and pepper
   6 Tbsp. extra-virgin olive oil
   1 pound red beets and 1/2 pound carrots, peeled and grated
   1/2 C. thinly sliced basil leaves.

In a large bowl, combine vinegar, lime juice, sugar, and salt and pepper to taste. Whisk to combine and whisk in oil. Add beets, carrots, basil, and parsley. Toss to mix and serve.

∼

**HUMMUS**
   3 1/2 C. canned OR soaked and cooked chickpeas/garbanzo beans
   1 Tbsp. baking soda (optional to help skin the chickpeas, then rinse away—see directions below)
   1/3 C. tahini paste
   8 roasted garlic cloves or more to taste (or substitute 1-3 fresh garlic cloves if you prefer a stronger sharper flavor)
   1/4 C. fresh lemon juice or more to taste
   1 Tbsp. extra virgin olive oil plus more for garnish 3/4 tsp. cumin
   1/2 tsp. salt or more to taste Pinch of cayenne pepper
   Paprika and fresh minced parsley for garnish if desired.
**Directions**
   1. If using canned chickpeas, drain and rinse. When cooking the

beans, follow soaking and cooking instructions. Drain after cooking and let them cool to room temperature.

2. To make hummus creamier, peel the cooked chickpeas. To remove the skins easily, place them in a skillet with 1 Tbsp. baking soda and stir, coating the beans thoroughly with baking soda. Heat up the skillet to medium, stirring the beans constantly, for 2-3 minutes until they are completely heated throughout and the skins begin to separate from the beans.

3. Reserve 15-20 whole chickpeas for garnish. If using a food processor, add a blade attachment. Place chickpeas, tahini paste, roasted garlic, lemon juice, 1 tbsp. olive oil, salt, cumin, and cayenne pepper into the processor. Process the mixture until it becomes a smooth, creamy hummus.

4. Taste the mixture and add more salt, lemon juice, or garlic to taste. Process again to blend any additional ingredients. If the texture seems too thick, add lukewarm water and continue processing until desired consistency is reached.

5. Transfer hummus to a shallow bowl and make a well in the center with a spoon.

6. Garnish with reserved chickpeas, a drizzle of olive oil, a sprinkle of paprika and fresh parsley. Serve with pita, crackers, or fresh vegetables.

∽

## SHAKSHUKA

(Eggs baked in tomato-red pepper sauce is a beloved Israeli breakfast.).

**Ingredients:**
3 Tbsp. extra-virgin olive oil
1 large onion thinly sliced
1 large red bell pepper, seeded and thinly sliced
3 garlic cloves, thinly sliced
1 tsp. ground cumin
1 tsp. paprika

1/8 tsp. ground cayenne, or to taste

1 (28-ounce) can whole plum tomatoes coarsely chopped with juice.

3/4 tsp. salt or more to taste.

1/4 tsp. black pepper or more to taste.

5 ounces feta cheese, crumbled (about 1 1/4 cups)

6 large eggs

Chopped cilantro

Hot sauce

**Directions**

1. Heat oven to 375 degrees F. Heat oil in a large skillet over medium-low.

2. Add onion and bell pepper. Cook gently until soft, about 20 minutes.

3. Add garlic and cook until tender, 1 to 2 minutes. Stir in cumin, paprika and cayenne, and cook for 1 minute.

4. Pour in tomatoes and season with 3/4 tsp. salt and 1/4 tsp. pepper. Simmer until tomatoes thicken, about 10 minutes. Add more salt and pepper to taste if needed. Stir in crumbled feta.

5. Gently crack eggs into skillet over tomatoes. Season eggs with salt and pepper. Transfer skillet to oven and bake until eggs are set, 7 to 10 minutes.

6. Sprinkle with cilantro and serve with hot sauce. To make it dairy free, leave out the feta and replace it with halved and pitted Kalamata olives on the top.

∽

## TABOULI/TABBOULEH

This is a refreshing, highly nutritious Middle Eastern salad made primarily of finely chopped parsley as the main ingredient along with tomatoes, mint, onion, bulgur wheat, and seasoned with olive oil, lemon juice, salt, and pepper. Bulgur (sometimes spelled bulghur) is whole wheat that has been cracked, cleaned, parboiled (or steamed), dried and then ground into desired sizes. Other variations include adding garlic or lettuce or semolina or quinoa in place of the wheat.

∼

## TAHINI

Tahini (sesame seed sauce) is a delicious paste made from ground-up hulled sesame seeds, a staple in the Mediterranean and Middle East. Its nutty taste is the binding agent in hummus besides being a marinade, cooking sauce, and/or salad dressing.

2 garlic cloves
1/2 tsp. fine sea salt
1/2 C. well-stirred tahini (sesame paste)
1/3 C. fresh lemon juice.
1/4 C. water
1/4 C. olive oil
1 Tbsp. finely chopped fresh cilantro
1 Tbsp. finely chopped fresh flat-leaf parsley

**Directions**

1. Marinate the garlic in lemon juice for 10 minutes. The acid in the lemon juice prevents the garlic from becoming too harsh and the lemon juice is infused with delicious, mellow garlic flavor.

2. Strain the garlic out of the lemon juice to ensure smooth tahini sauce that prevents the garlic flavor from dominating. Skip the garlic if you prefer and add the lemon juice as you whisk in the tahini, salt, and cumin.

3. Whisk in ice water until the mixture is smooth and creamy. When tahini is added to the bowl, it thickens but will loosen later when enough ice water is added.

4. Adjust to taste. Add more water for a thinner consistency, more salt if desired, and/or more lemon juice for extra tang. Tahini sauce is rich, creamy, smooth, nutty, and tangy. The subtle garlic flavor enhances the toasted sesame. It is excellent as a dipping sauce, paired with lamb, or spread on sandwiches.

## HALVA OR SESAME SEED-HONEY CANDIES

Many say this healthy, nutritious treat originated in Greece where it is called Pastelli, but I discovered and fell in love with it all over Israel. Recipe variations are found throughout Middle Eastern, Mediterranean, Indian, and Asian nations. The final texture can be fluffy, fudge-like, or any desired consistency in between. Added flavors can include vanilla, chocolate, caramel, and more. Or create nougats by adding roasted almonds, walnuts, pistachios, hazelnuts, macadamia or any other nuts along with whipped egg whites and sometimes chopped candied fruits. All of these options are nutritious and delicious!

**Ingredients**

1 C. raw or toasted white sesame seeds.

1 C. honey.

Add a bit of white sugar if the desired end result is to be hard instead of chewy.

**Directions**

1. In a large, greased pot, bring the honey to a boil for 5 minutes.

2. Meanwhile, toast the raw sesame seeds in a sauté pan for several minutes until golden brown unless they're already toasted.

3. Once the honey is bubbling and the seeds are toasted, add the seeds to the honey mixture and boil again to thicken, about 10 minutes, stirring occasionally.

4. Carefully pour the hot candy mixture in a thin layer onto a greased parchment paper-lined baking dish or cookie sheet.

5. Allow to cool at room temperature before cutting into squares or bars.

**OR**

1. In a large skillet over low heat, lightly toast the sesame seeds until fragrant (about 2-3 minutes).

2. Heat the honey and salt in a saucepan over low heat. When it has thickened (after about 5 minutes), stir in the sesame seeds and bring to a boil.

3. Line a baking sheet with parchment paper and spray with cooking spray. Pour the hot mixture onto the parchment and spread it out to a 1/4-inch thickness. Be careful; it will be hot.

4. Leave the pasteli out on the baking parchment until it comes to room temperature. When cool, use a knife to cut it into pieces.

5. Store in an airtight container, with parchment paper in between layers of candy. Kept in a cool, dry place, it stores well.

Note: Adding up to about 1/4 C. sugar during cooking creates a harder, crispier candy. Without sugar, the candy stays chewy.

This recipe is delicious, but may be varied by adding cinnamon, lemon, orange zest, or ginger.

**Things To Do**

- Do enjoy foreign foods. Taste the foods you are offered and express enjoyment and appreciation, especially when receiving hospitality.
- Do inquire about the ingredients used in foreign dishes if you have serious food allergies so you do not encounter any problem surprises.

**Things Not To Do**

- Do not disapprove of or disdain of foods offered or any cultural practices observed, despite your personal opinion. Do always be a gracious guest.

# ADDENDUM

### Photo Options

Sadly, few of my many personal photos are of sufficient digital quality to print. I also learned that including many in this book would double the publication cost. However, excellent photos of nearly all locations and destinations can easily be found online these days. Reprint permission for photos you find and like on the Department of Tourism site may be requested at https://goisrael.com. Therefore, I'm not including a photo section in this book but will post occasional pictures plus regular blog updates sharing news of my other books and travels on my delorestopliff.com website. I will hope to see you there.

### Maps and Resources

I've selected the map provided at the front of this book as the one most helpful of those I've examined. It helps readers and travelers find their way to recognize major cities, sites, territories, and natural geographic features. Those who desire more detailed map

*Addendum*

information may also contact the Israel Department of Tourism at https://www.gov.il/en

**Glossary Terms**

**Aliyah**—Under the Law of Return, Jews from around the world are welcomed home to Israel as residents who eventually become citizens.

**Bar/Bat Mitzvah**—the traditional religious initiation ceremony for Jewish boys or girls respectively when they reach age of 12 (13 in some places), equipping them to observe religious precepts and take part in public worship.

**Decapolis**—ten cities in Israel's northeastern edge from the first centuries BC/BCE to AD/CE. The Gospels mention them frequently.

**Eretz Israel**—literally, *The Land of Israel.*

**Gentiles**—non-Jewish people. (Goyim is the derogatory form).

**Kibbutz**—a collectively owned town or settlement traditionally based on agriculture.

**Knesset**—Israel's national unicameral legislature.

**Mishnah**—the oral tradition of Jewish law forming the first part of the Talmud.

**Moshav**—an Israeli cooperative town or settlement made up of privately owned individual farms.

**Old Hebrew Script**—dates to at least the sixth century B.C.E. and is all consonants, no vowels.

**Pentateuch**—the first five books of the Hebrew Bible, Genesis, Exodus, Leviticus, Numbers, Deuteronomy—the same as the Torah

**Shabbat/Sabbath**—Judaism's seventh day of the week for rest and prayer from sundown Friday to sundown Saturday.

**Shalom**—Peace.

**Talmud**—The Talmud consists of the Mishnah, the oral tradition of Jewish law, and the Gemara, its written rabbinical commentary.

**Torah**—the first five books of the Hebrew Bible, Genesis, Exodus, Leviticus, Numbers, Deuteronomy, the same as the Pentateuch.

*Addendum*

**Ulpan**—a school or institute for teaching basic Hebrew language skills especially for Israel's immigrants.

## Additional Reading

Bibleplaces.com – an excellent online source of information on major biblical sites.

International Standard Bible Encyclopedia (ISBE)

The Jewish Website Aish Hatorah - https://www.aish.com/

Books written by famed American Archaeologist, Rabbi Nelson Glueck, especially *Rivers in the Desert, The Other Side of Jordan, The Excavations of Solomon's Seaport*.

Old Hebrew Language - https://www.biblicalarchaeology.org/daily/biblical-artifacts/inscriptions/the-story-of-the-old-hebrew-script/?mqsc=E4134975&dk=ZE1380ZF0&utm_source=WhatCountsEmail&utm_medium=BHDA%20Daily%20Newsletter&utm_campaign=8_9_21_Educational_Opportunities

Pella, Jordan – where Christians fled - https://www.biblicalarchaeology.org/daily/biblical-sites-places/biblical-archaeology-places/pella-a-window-on-survival/?mqsc=E4134958&dk=ZE1280ZF0&utm_source=WhatCountsE-mail&utm_medium=BHDA%20Week%20in%20Review&utm_-campaign=8_7_21_From_Judah_to_Edom_Week_in_Review

*Excavating Ancient Pella, Jordan: Archaeology Investigates the Jerusalem Christians' Escape to Pella"* in Bible History Daily.

When it's not possible to visit Israel because of personal situations or conditions like Covid variants, free livestream and Zoom tours are increasingly available. One offered through Jerusalem Tours International is currently at this link https://www.israel365.com/virtual-pilgrimage-to-israel/

This *Smithsonian Magazine* link presents the discovery and development of Magdala, the newest and excellent restoration from the days of Jesus on the Sea of Galilee https://www.smithsonianmag.com/history/unearthing-world-jesus-180957515/

*Addendum*

For fellowship opportunities in and around Jerusalem and throughout Israel, message me privately at delorestopliff.com or Delores Topliff Books on Facebook.

| ENGLISH | HEBREW | ARABIC |
| --- | --- | --- |
| All the honor to you! | Kol Hakavod | Kol alehtiram |
| Do you speak English? | Ata medaber Anglit? | Hal tatakalam al-lughat Al'iinjlizia |
| Thank you/thank you very much | Todah/towdah roba | Shukran |
| You're welcome | Boker tov | Afwan |
| Sorry/excuse me | Slicha | Āsif! |
| How to get to.? | Eich Magi'im le...? | Saeiduni fi aleuthur ala... |
| Hello/goodbye | Shalom | Salaam |
| See you later | Lehitraot | 'Arak lahiqaan |
| Good night | Layla tov | Tusbih ealaa khayr |
| What is your name? | Eych korim lecha? | Sho ismak? |
| Nice to meet you | Nayim Mayod | Tasharefet bema're-fatek |
| Have a nice day | Yom tov | Atmna lk ywma tyb |
| What time is it? | Ma hasha'a? | 'Aya saea |
| How much does this cost? | Kama ze ole? | Kam yukalif hdha |
| Please | Bevakasha | Min faDlikl |
| The bill, please | Cheshbon, bevakasha | Alhesab min fadlik |
| How are you? | Ma nishma? | Kayf halik |

# MORE OF DELORES TOPLIFF'S BOOKS

Thank you for reading *A Traveling Grandma's Guide to Israel: Adventures, Wit, and Wisdom*. If you enjoyed it, look for Delores's novels published by Scrivenings Press:

*Books Afloat* and *Strong Currents*, Books 1 and 2 in her WWII Columbia River Undercurrents series

*Wilderness Wife*, based on the heroic life of abandoned single mother Marguerite McKay, later Mrs. Dr. John McLoughlin on the North American Frontier in the early 1800s

*Christmas Tree Wars*, a fun romantic suspense involving two competing Wisconsin Christmas tree growers in a contest to provide the White House Christmas Tree to be decorated by First Lady Bird Johnson.

Also look for her four children's pictures books, two of which won first prize in international contests:

*Whoosh*
*Little Big Chief and the Bear Hunt, Little Chief and Ogopogo,*
*Woodsy, the Wonder Bear*

All are available on Amazon.

*More of Delores Topliff's books*

*More of Delores Topliff's books*

*More of Delores Topliff's books*

## More of Delores Topliff's books

# FROM THE AUTHOR

I was teaching in a small college when Bob Allen, a retired archaeologist, came to visit. I had just agreed to develop an archaeology course but had few resources. Bob insisted on sending books, color slides, replicas, and several genuine artifacts. He donated $3,000 to our college IF I would travel to Israel to study hands-on. That 36-day trip changed my life. I loved Israel and its people so much, I worked hard to send myself eight more times. I stayed in touch with friends, learned lots, and had fun. Many people asked me to help plan their trips. This book resulted. There's not another one like it. Read and enjoy whether you prefer armchair adventures or plan your own journeys.

Besides writing and speaking, I teach online in a Minnesota university. I spend half of each year on my family's Minnesota farm and the other half in Mississippi enjoying its balmy climate and gentle people. Travel is my favorite means of learning. I keep my passport ready and advise others to do the same.

*From the Author*

**Connect with and follow Delores on these sites:**

- Website: https://delorestopliff.com
- Blog: https://delorestopliff.com/blog/
- Facebook: https://www.facebook.com/DETopliff
- Twitter: @delorestopliff
- Instagram: delorese.topliff
- Pinterest: @delorestopliff
- Or feel free to email her at dtopliff@yahoo.com.

www.ingramcontent.com/pod-product-compliance
Lightning Source LLC
Chambersburg PA
CBHW071342080526
44587CB00017B/2928